THESE TWELVE

THESE TWELVE

The Gospel Through the Apostles' Eyes

ROD BENNETT

Published by Catholic Answers, Inc.
2020 Gillespie Way
El Cajon, California 92020
1-888-291-8000 orders
619-387-0042 fax
catholic.com

Printed in the United States of America

Cover and interior design: Claudine Mansour Design
Cover painting: *Christ and the Twelve Apostles*, by Taddeo di Bartolo, ca. 1400, Courtesy of The Metropolitan Museum of Art

978-1-68357-255-8
978-1-68357-256-5 Kindle
978-1-68357-257-2 ePub

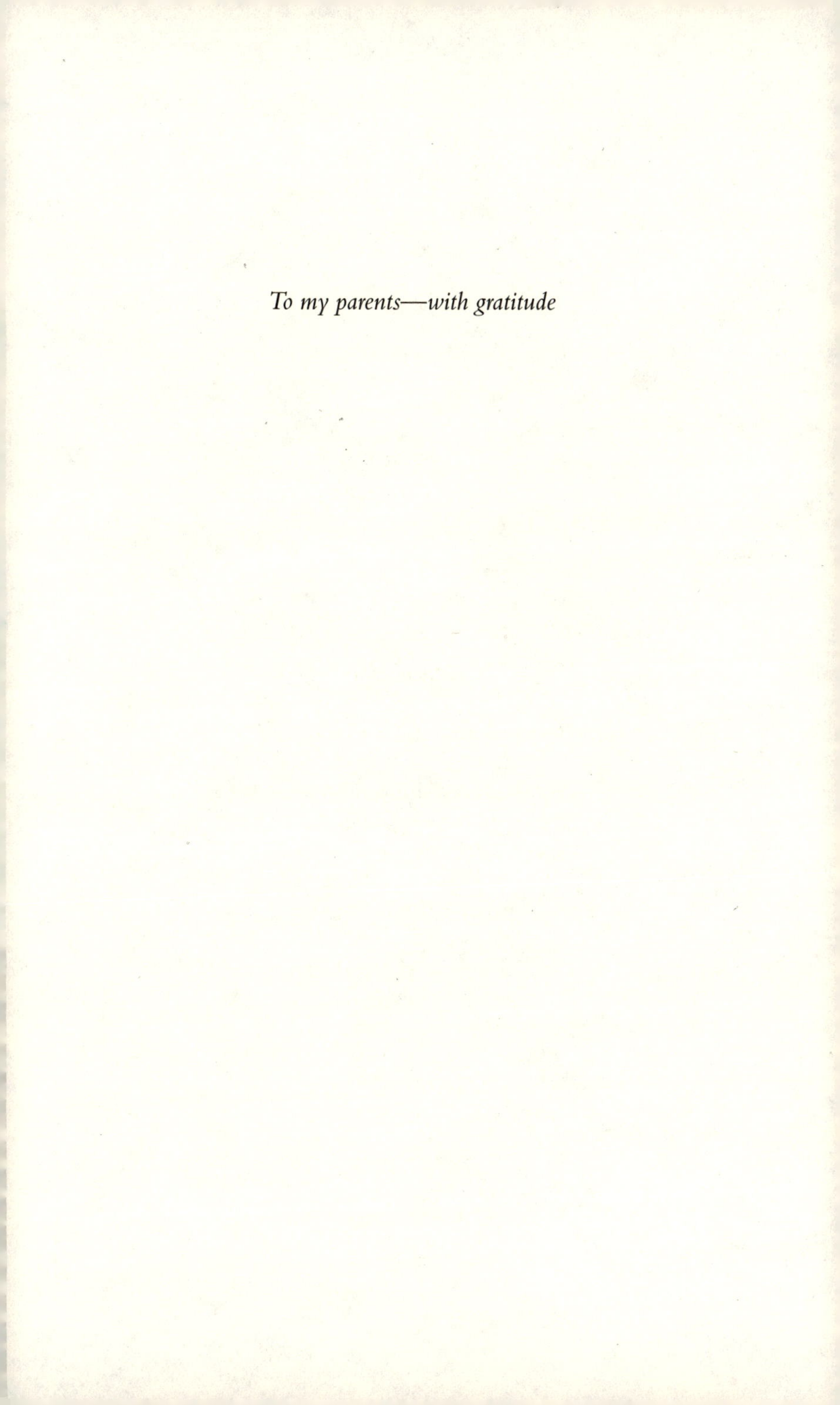

To my parents—with gratitude

CONTENTS

Introduction

ONE APOSTOLIC CHURCH

"These twelve Jesus sent out."

—MATTHEW 10:5

What was it like to become one of the twelve apostles?

What did "the Jesus experience" look like, feel like, from the *inside*?

How did it change the chosen twelve—and how did they understand what had happened to them afterward?

I first began to ponder this spiritual thought experiment back in the 1980s, while still an Evangelical Christian just returned from the short-term mission field. I'd recently fallen in love with the writings of C.S. Lewis, that imaginative Anglican apologist who had taken to the media in defense of what he called "mere Christianity." But though he had managed somehow to gain the stamp of approval from my Evangelical gatekeepers, making me feel safe reading him, it didn't take me long to realize that Lewis had some . . . eccentricities.

He didn't like labels himself, and I wouldn't have known what "Anglo-Catholic" meant at the time anyway, but watching Lewis write in defense of the dogma of purgatory and hearing him comfortably employ expressions like "Our

Lady" and "the Blessed Sacrament" certainly opened the door to new ideas and new questions.

The term *High Church* is sometimes used; and Lewis definitely did have a higher view of the Church than I was accustomed to. Among other things, he wrote this in his popular essay *God in the Dock*, "If there is anything in the teaching of the New Testament which is in the nature of a command, it is that you are obliged to take the Sacrament (John vi. 53-54: 'Except ye eat the flesh of the Son of man, and drink his blood, ye have no life in you. Whoso eateth my flesh, and drinketh my blood, hath eternal life; and I will raise him up at the last day') and you can't do it without going to Church." Most pertinently here, Lewis accepted and defended the Nicene Creed, with its strange (to me, thus far) confession that "We believe in one holy, catholic, and apostolic Church."

Let us pass over that word *catholic* for the time being. What did *apostolic* mean in this context?

I vividly remember asking a friend of mine, a bright Baptist seminarian, during a memorable walk along a Florida beach as part of a church retreat. "Oh, the apostles were nothing," he said. "No special role at all, other than allowing themselves to become the medium by which God wrote the New Testament. They just happened to be the first generation of Christian disciples, that's all." His curt, preemptive dismissal of the whole topic, I'm afraid, just made me the more curious.

This book represents the fruit of forty years of that curiosity, meditations on my part in response to that unexpectedly testy answer. I've written it up for the use of anyone else who might be wondering about such things.

For lifelong Catholics (and also members of the other liturgical communions), accustomed to reciting the creeds and to keeping feast days dedicated to the apostles and worshipping at parishes named after them, the apostolicity of the Church may seem commonplace. But for Evangelicals like my friend, any attempt to assign a group of mere mortals like ourselves to such a central role in the economy of our Faith has always set off alarm bells.

Born out of the horrific wars of religion that so perplexed and demoralized Christian Europe in the seventeenth century, today's Evangelical groups (theological successors of the Anabaptists and the radical Reformation) were consciously created to reduce human instrumentalities in God's plan of salvation to an absolute minimum. Confidence in tainted man, touched by the Holy Spirit or not, had reached rock bottom; and the result has been an intense 500-year effort to cut out the middle man and get one's gospel, as far as possible, directly from God alone. And this had been my own starting point as much as my friend's.

Could God have saved us by means of the Bible alone? Of course he could have—just as he could have saved us by one snap of his cosmic fingers; not only without the apostles but without the Incarnation for that matter. But is that how he actually chose to work out his will? Is that the kind of salvation actually recorded in the Bible itself? As I found Lewis avowing that his celebrated apologetics had been "based on the divinity of Christ, the truth of the creeds, and the authority of the Christian tradition" and then moved on to the writers who had influenced Lewis's own change of perspective (writers such as J.R.R. Tolkien and G.K. Chesterton), I conceived a desire to re-read the Gospels through a different pair of spectacles—or, at least, without the jaundice-yellow set fashioned for me during my Anabaptist youth.

These Twelve is certainly nothing so ambitious as a life of Christ; so please don't be surprised to find me leaving out many of the most famous scenes and neglecting important parts of the larger story. It's more in the nature of a *flyover*, as it were, highlighting a few perhaps neglected connections within the narrative that might possibly have some bearing on the issues in question.

Like the author of *The Chronicles of Narnia* and *Out of the Silent Planet*, imagination is as central to my life and work as the more conventional theological or devotional part. So I hope you won't be surprised to see me make one or two imaginative leaps in these pages—educated guesses, I suppose, at biographical details lost to the wreck of the ages—in my efforts to connect some of the dots. I have cited Scripture and the early Fathers extensively along the way in an effort to keep at least one foot on the ground. But, if you take the book as one more layman's effort (and C.S. Lewis was perhaps the most celebrated Christian layman of the twentieth century) to engage *your* imagination on the subject, too—rather than an attempt at genuine scholarship—I expect you'll do fine.

So now, let's walk a mile or two in the apostolic sandals, so to speak . . . and see where the pathway takes us.

—Rod Bennett
Tarifftown, Tennessee

THESE TWELVE

1
THE FIG TREE

"Like grapes in the wilderness, I found Israel.
Like the first fruit on the fig tree,
in its first season, I saw your ancestors."

—Hosea 9:10

Imagine a young man of faith, a Hebrew adhering to the age-old religion of the Hebrews in the land of his forefathers; living, to be sure, a long time ago by human standards, yet a memory fresh as yesterday to his God and ours—he for whom "one day is like a thousand years, and a thousand years are like one day" (2 Pet. 3:8). Now imagine that young man lying on his back under the shady boughs of an enormous fig tree laden with slowly ripening fruit. Where the sun does penetrate the canopy, it dots the grassy carpet around him with dazzling miniature suns of yellow; when he gazes upward through the rustling leaves, azure glimpses of a Mediterranean sky offer a thousand tiny windows to infinity. If he pauses to cast a sidelong gaze at the things of earth, he can see, a mere half-mile distant down a long sloping hillside, the shimmering blue expanse of what St. Mark will call the Sea of Galilee the rough, rural people of the north know as Lake Gennesaret.

His father Tolmai seems to have named him for a somewhat obscure biblical figure: Nathan-el, son of Jesse, one of King David's older brothers (1 Chron. 2:14). Perhaps Tolmai "meant him for the church," so to speak, as English fathers in the novels of Jane Austen sometimes do with sons too weak for war and too unworldly for politics. There's an old tradition, at any rate, that Tolmai's Nathanael[1] was studying to be a scribe (Judaism's version of a canon lawyer) before a greater call interrupted his career. That Nathanael's one big moment in the Gospels centers around a fig tree may add credence to this extrabiblical notice, since we do know for a fact that several prominent rabbis of the era, such as the famous apocalyptic revolutionist Akiba Ben Joseph, did choose the shade of Israel's many large fig trees as their islands of solitude for daily prayer and spiritual reading. This may, in fact, have been a traditional practice for Hebrew clerics of the day.

Like the Pharisees with whom they are so closely associated, the scribes majored in the Law; on *Torah* that is—the five books of Moses to whom God revealed his marching orders for mankind. Nathanael's textbooks would, therefore, have been hand-copied biblical scrolls much too expensive for the average layman to easily access but loaned out by the synagogues as core curriculum for rabbinical students. And though these five sacred books—Genesis, Exodus, Leviticus, Numbers, and Deuteronomy—contain much more than just law, studying the Mosaic statutes and learning to enforce them rigorously upon the faithful was certainly the job at

1 John's Gospel mentions Nathanael but not Bartholomew; the other three Gospels name Bartholomew but never Nathanael. The synoptics always list Philip and Bartholomew together; and John tells us it was Philip who brought a Galilean friend named Nathanael to Jesus. These facts, among others, have led many scholars to the conclusion that "Bartholomew" is actually a patronymic—a surname, that is, meaning "Son of Tholomai" (Tholomeus), just as Bartimaeus is the "son of Timaeus" (Mark 10:46).

hand for a scribe in the making. Many of what we might consider purely civic duties fell upon the scribes as well in that theocratic society: the drafting of marriage contracts, issuing bills of divorcement, the drawing up of deeds, wills, mortgages, and so forth. Some of the nation's leaders were so fixated on law that they neglected or even actively denigrated the rest of the Hebrew sacred writings—the books of history, wisdom, and prophecy that make up the remainder of what we Christians call the Old Testament. The party of the Sadducees, in fact—the "liturgy police" of their era and among those who actually performed all of the elaborate rituals mandated by the *Torah*—doubted that any books besides these original five had received divine inspiration at all.

Nathanael's chosen vocation, in short, was heavily focused on the "thou shalts" and "thou shalt nots" of Jewish life, not so much on the mystic or more inspiring side of the Faith as it existed at that time.

By the time we meet him in Scripture, however, Nathanael's thoughts seem already to have wandered elsewhere—away from the dry duties of religion to become steeped instead in the symbolic metaphors of his nation's folklore and the prophetic reveries of her seers. Even though the Bible gives us only two real clues to work with, both of those two—a personal friendship and a handful of short sayings, several of which display spiritual weariness and a growing cynicism—show a man looking no longer for law but for salvation; for the personal and national salvation that the Jews, more and more as the centuries progressed, had come to associate with belief in a *new Moses*, a long-expected Deliverer: *Melech HaMoshiach,* the Messiah, the chosen king who was to come.

Just the tree itself and the fruit hanging on it would have been enough to send such a man's thoughts back to the prophets and patriarchs. Ripe figs such as these had been part of the produce of the land that the two faithful spies, Joshua and Caleb, brought back from Canaan, and which they used to encourage God's people to press on in faith and to enter the Promised Land to begin with (see Numbers 13). During Solomon's reign, the fig tree served as an icon of the peace and prosperity that had come to the nation under the house of David and would, by means of continued obedience and faith, be her portion forever:

> Judah and Israel were as numerous as the sand by the sea; they ate and drank and were happy. Solomon was sovereign over all the kingdoms from the Euphrates to the land of the Philistines, even to the border of Egypt; they brought tribute and served Solomon all the days of his life. During Solomon's lifetime Judah and Israel lived in safety, from Dan even to Beer-sheba, all of them under their own vines and fig trees (1 Kings 4:20-21, 25).

There had also been a fig tree in the garden of Solomon's great love poem, the Song of Songs, in which Israel was, symbolically speaking, to have reveled in a perpetual springtime of conjugal intimacy with her divine bridegroom (2:13). Yet fig leaves, it must not be forgotten, had covered the nakedness of Adam and Eve as well, after they were expelled from another garden on account of their sins, cut off from access to life and peace by God's own angel of judgment. And Nathanael, it seems, may have been wondering whether *this* image, of the two, was really the more pertinent to his current situation.

God's chosen nation was certainly *not* where she had been in the glory days of King Solomon or even during the more recent post-exilic restoration under Zerubbabel,

Nehemiah, and Ezra. The current king, here in the late twenties after the birth of Christ, was Herod Antipas, a godless pretender; no descendant of the Davidic kings at all, truly sovereign over nothing, but merely a puppet of the conquering Romans. The "peace" he guaranteed was a mockery. Judah and Israel (divided, as during our own Civil War, into two hostile camps, the Jews of the south and the Samaritans in the north) threatened to renew hostilities at any moment; and Judea was itself riven into violent political factions, each full of hatred for all the others. Even the clerical caste to which Nathanael was aspiring seemed rotten and moribund at times.

Then, quite apart from the rival parties to which we have already alluded, the once-idealistic, theologically orthodox body of the Pharisees had fallen on sad, distressing times. Every day, it seemed, there came to light some new scandal, some new revelation about a prominent cleric mixed up in financial chicanery or sexual immorality. God had promised David a kingdom that would never fail and that a man of David's own bloodline would sit on its throne forever (2 Sam. 7:10-14).

And yet David's kingdom had failed, had it not? Most of his successors (even before the Davidic line collapsed completely during the Babylonian captivity) had been feckless wastrels when they weren't, as Ahab and Manasseh were, virtual devils in human form. And now it was visibly failing again, was it not? What then of God's promise to David? The fig leaves of denial, like the sham coverings with which our first parents sought pathetically to deceive him who cannot be deceived, seemed to be Israel's only answer everywhere.

Yet whenever Nathanael's thoughts turned to the nation's failings in this way, the memory of his own faults seems to have sprung quickly to mind in their wake. After all, what had *he* sacrificed to save the nation? Who was *he* to criticize, who had never borne the heat of battle? "Toward the scorners he is scornful," went the old Proverb, "but to the humble he gives favor" (3:34). The fig tree, after all, was a place of confession as much as any other kind of prayer. He would not deny his anguish and perplexity, any more than the prophet Habakkuk had denied his own when he compared Judah to a fig tree sick and dying: "Though the fig tree does not blossom, and no fruit is on the vines; though the produce of the olive fails, and the fields yield no food; though the flock is cut off from the fold, and there is no herd in the stalls, yet I will rejoice in the Lord; I will exult in the God of my salvation" (Hab. 3:17–18). That was the proper note! Woe and lament, yes—but trust as well; trust in *Yahweh Yireh,* the "God who provides," called thusly by our father Abraham when God himself provided a lamb to sacrifice in place of Isaac, the beloved son. The note of hope.

And this note of hope, as Nathanael well knew, had always been connected with the holy rumor of the coming Messiah—and also, curiously enough, with the image of the fig tree. "In days to come," wrote the prophet Micah,

> the mountain of the Lord's house[2] shall be established as the highest of the mountains, and shall be raised up above the hills. Peoples shall stream to it, and many nations shall come and say: "Come, let us go up to the mountain of the Lord, to the house of the God of Jacob; that he may teach us his ways and that we may walk in his paths." For out of Zion shall go forth instruction,

2 A reference to Mt. Zion, where the city of Jerusalem stands and where the Temple built by David's son Solomon once stood.

> and the word of the Lord from Jerusalem. He shall judge between many peoples, and shall arbitrate between strong nations far away; they shall beat their swords into plowshares, and their spears into pruning hooks, nation shall not lift up sword against nation, neither shall they learn war any more; but they shall all sit under their own vines and under their own fig trees, and no one shall make them afraid; for the mouth of the Lord of hosts has spoken (Mic. 4:1-4).

It may be that Nathanael took, from time to time, an encouraging bit of extracurricular reading along these lines to his secret place of prayer; the prophecy of Isaiah, perhaps, or one of the Psalms:

> Why do the nations conspire, and the peoples plot in vain? The kings of the earth set themselves, and the rulers take counsel together, against the Lord and his anointed, saying, "Let us burst their bonds asunder, and cast their cords from us." He who sits in the heavens laughs; the Lord has them in derision. Then he will speak to them in his wrath, and terrify them in his fury, saying, "I have set my king on Zion, my holy hill." I will tell of the decree of the Lord: he said to me, "You are my son; today I have begotten you. Ask of me, and I will make the nations your heritage, and the ends of the earth your possession. You shall break them with a rod of iron, and dash them in pieces like a potter's vessel" (Ps. 2:1-9).

A son of God coming to set things right! What Jewish heart wouldn't skip a beat at such an astounding image? And had not the great prophet of Judah lifted this conception to heights even more amazing?[3]

> The people who walked in darkness have seen a great light . . . they rejoice before you as with joy at the harvest, as people exult when dividing plunder. For the yoke of their burden, and the bar across their shoulders, the rod of their oppressor, you have broken as on the day of Midian. For all the boots of the tramping warriors and all the garments rolled in blood shall be burned as fuel for the fire. For a child has been born for us, a son given to us; authority rests upon his shoulders; and he is named Wonderful Counselor, Mighty God, Everlasting Father, Prince of Peace. His authority shall grow continually, and there shall be endless peace for the throne of David and his kingdom. He will establish and uphold it with justice and with righteousness from this time onward and forevermore. The zeal of the Lord of hosts will do this (Isa. 9:1, 3-7).

Isaiah's prophecy was startling, to say the least, and certainly inspiring; but also, as Nathanael had noticed in the case of so many other such prophecies, very confusing . . . if not downright self-contradictory. He was convinced, for instance, that the prophet's reference to "the day of Midian" was an evocation of Gideon from the book of Judges, one of Israel's great military deliverers of the past.[4] A second

3 The Hellenistic scribe Ben Sira refers to Isaiah as "the great spirit . . . who revealed what was to occur to the end of time, and the hidden things before they happened" (Sir. 48:24-45).

4 The Battle of Midian is depicted in Judges chapters 6 and 7.

Gideon, he was sure, would have no trouble at all casting off the cords of Rome and terrifying Herod with God's fury.

What was less clear was how such a simple man of war (however used by God) might be fittingly referred to as "Wonderful Counselor" or "Prince of Peace"—let alone God's "begotten son" or the nation's "Everlasting Father." Not even Moses himself had merited honorifics like these! Elsewhere, Isaiah says that the Messiah would make "intercession for the transgressors" (53:12,) not slay them; and he was destined to carry away "the iniquity of us all" (53:6). In passages such as these, the great prophet could sound more like Zechariah or Hosea, who spoke of Messiah as "lowly, and riding upon an ass" (Zech. 9:9)—the symbol of a peacemaker, like an emissary waving the white flag of truce—and as one who would draw men to himself "with bands of love" (Hos. 11:4). But then a few chapters later, Isaiah returns blithely to his blood-and-thunder motif, depicting a Deliverer who can say, "I trod them in my anger and trampled them in my wrath; their juice spattered on my garments, and stained all my robes. For the day of vengeance was in my heart, and the year for my redeeming work had come . . . I trampled down peoples in my anger, I crushed them in my wrath, and I poured out their lifeblood on the earth" (Isa. 63:3-4, 6). Messianic prophecies were heartening, to be sure, but Nathanael probably wondered why the prophets couldn't be just a bit more . . . *straightforward* than they ever seemed willing to be.

Our second reason for deducing that Nathanael rather specialized in this field of study is that personal friendship we mentioned a moment ago: his acquaintance with Philip of Bethsaida, who was a known associate of *Yokhanan Bar-Zekharyah*, commonly called John the Baptist, the wild-eyed prophet of Bethabara. It seems probable, in fact, that Nathanael initiated and consciously cultivated an association with Philip—perhaps at one of the Baptist's mass preaching events—precisely in order to get closer to John and to understand him better.[5] Our "messianic investigator" may even have accepted John's baptism of repentance by this point, as Philip undoubtedly had; the Bible doesn't say one way or the other. If so, Nathanael had his own memories of John to reflect on, there in his shady oasis by the sea.

Of all the many contenders for the title who seemed to come down the pike in those turbulent times, John the Baptist had been by far the most *plausible-looking* Messiah. Nathanael may have had personal recollections of the "shepherd king" Arthrongeus, who led a closely watched insurrection against the Romans during the reign of Herod's brother Archelaus. Like Judas Maccabeus (another of the Bible's heroic military saviors[6]) he had four tall, manly brothers who followed him on his great crusade and became generals in his militias. Alas, Arthrongeus spoiled his look for the role by turning to mere plunder in the end—a messiah for personal gain. Nathanael probably also studied the career of Simon of Peraea, a former slave in Herod's household whose bloody uprising appears to have taken place when our subject was a small boy. Simon, too, had made an impressive showing for a while, raising the hopes of many when a group of notable supporters put a diadem on his head and declared him king of the Jews. Yet Simon ultimately disappointed as well, ending his campaign with a whimper rather than a bang.

5 Philip may or may not have been an actual disciple of John the Baptist but he certainly was close to two of John's disciples, Andrew and Simon Bar Jonas. John baptized at Bethabara in Judea, about eighty miles south of Cana. If Nathanael traveled there to hear him, he may have recognized a familiar Galilean accent in Philip and approached him for more information.

6 The story of Judas and his four brothers and their revolt against the alien Seleucid Empire during the second century B.C. is covered in the two deuterocanonical books 1 and 2 Maccabees.

After a series of reverses, he slunk away like a coward, before being caught in a trap and beheaded by Gratus, Herod's captain of the guard.[7] The Baptist, however, was *not* a disappointment—very far from it—even though, as our story will show, Nathanael had already rejected him, perhaps reluctantly, at least in regard to any thought of messiahship.

For one thing, there was the constantly whispered story about a miraculous birth. His mother, Elizabeth, it was said, had been—like Sarah herself, mother of the whole Hebrew people—well past childbearing years at the time of John's delivery. The Baptist himself never trumpeted the tale, of course, but one heard it repeated everywhere, often from individuals in a position to know. And then the adult John simply *looked* like a character stepped out of Scripture; in fact, his appearance and his lifestyle were exactly those of the mighty prophet Elijah as described in the second book of Kings—"He wore a garment of haircloth, with a girdle of leather about his loins" (1:8)—and he lived off the land in the wilderness east of Jordan.

None of this had gone unnoticed by those who remembered the messianic prophecies of Malachi, written 400 years earlier: "Behold, I will send you Elijah the prophet before the great and terrible day of the LORD comes. And he will turn the hearts of fathers to their children and the hearts of children to their fathers, lest I come and smite the land with a curse" (Mic. 4:5-6). Since, according to 2 Kings 2:1-12, Elijah never actually died but was carried up to heaven alive in a chariot of fire, Micah's prophecy was widely expected to be literally fulfilled—an actual "second coming of Elijah," so to speak. John's message had been that of Elijah as

7 The tales of Arthrongeus and Simon of Peraea are recorded in Josephus's *Antiquities of the Jews*.

well: a call to national repentance and a warning about the lateness of the hour. "He said to the multitudes that came out to be baptized by him . . . 'Who warned you to flee from the wrath to come? . . . Even now the axe is laid to the root of the trees; every tree therefore that does not bear good fruit is cut down and thrown into the fire'" (Luke 3:7, 9). No wonder the people, as St. Luke so mildly puts it, "were in expectation" and "questioned in their hearts concerning John, whether perhaps he were the Christ" (Luke 3:15). It is also possible that Nathanael was present at Bethabara himself the day Israel's "new Elijah" finally addressed the many rumors about his mission directly—the day John the Baptist, that is, officially *begged off.*

The Pharisees, it seems, had looked at John askance since the beginning. They always did with any prospective messiahs since such a claim, by its very nature, contained a dangerous political element; including the obvious implication that they themselves would have to swear obedience to such a man sooner or later. So, as St. John's Gospel tells us, "The Jews sent priests and Levites from Jerusalem to ask him, 'Who are you?'" (1:19)—a straight-up demand to hear the Baptist either confirm or deny. And though he doubtless knew very well that he was quashing the source of his own notoriety, John didn't hesitate:

> He confessed, he did not deny, but confessed, "I am not the Christ." And they asked him, "What then? Are you Elijah?" He said, "I am not." "Are you the prophet?" And he answered, "No." They said to him then, "Who are you? Let us have an answer for those who sent us. What do you say about yourself?" He said, "I am the voice of one crying in the wilderness, 'Make straight the way

> of the Lord,' as the prophet Isaiah said."[8] They asked him, "Then why are you baptizing, if you are neither the Christ, nor Elijah, nor the prophet?" John answered them, "I baptize with water; but among you stands one whom you do not know, even he who comes after me, the thong of whose sandal I am not worthy to untie" (John 1:19-27).

So it was back to the old drawing board then, as far as a man like Nathanael was concerned. John's addendum—the idea that the true Messiah "stood among" the Jews somewhere even as he spoke—sounded encouraging, of course; but Nathanael had long since learned that the symbolic language of imminence and expectation employed by the prophets often operated on an entirely inhuman timescale. What might sound like one day could, in a message from God, end up being a thousand years. Philip stayed with John, even after this deflating announcement, though Nathanael may have wondered why. Meanwhile, Nathanael . . . went back to his fig tree for more waiting.

There must have been hundreds like Nathanael in those days, in every land where Jews were dispersed, for Luke writes of two such waiting every day at the Temple. He tells us of Simeon, "righteous and devout," part of a faithful remnant "looking for the consolation of Israel"; and of Anna the prophetess who "gave thanks to God, and spoke of [the Messiah] to all who were awaiting the redemption of Jerusalem" (Luke 2:25, 38, NABRE). And all of these messianic "lookouts," surely, experienced the same kind of ups and downs, highs and lows. Their hearts thrilled to

8 Isaiah 40:3.

hear his voice in advance when they read Psalm 40: "Lo, I come; in the roll of the book it is written of me; I delight to do thy will, O my God . . . I have told the glad news of deliverance in the great congregation" (7, 9). But then, in a different mood, they turned to Psalm 102 instead; one of David's as-yet unanswered pleas for deliverance, one of his gut-honest cries of complaint that seem to border, at times, on presumption: "Do not hide thy face from me in the day of my distress! Incline thy ear to me; answer me speedily in the day when I call! . . . I eat ashes like bread, and mingle tears with my drink, because of thy indignation and anger; for thou hast taken me up and thrown me away. My days are like an evening shadow; I wither away like grass" (2, 9-11).

Those who continued, however, to read *all* the words of Psalm 102 experienced, as have so many others through the centuries, one of those *uncanny moments*—those holy, inexplicable non sequiturs wherein the Psalmist, at the height of his outrage, switches abruptly, almost unconsciously, to his *prophetic* voice, as if taken by a trance, possessed by a Spirit:

> But thou, O Lord, art enthroned for ever; thy name endures to all generations. Thou wilt arise and have pity on Zion; it is the time to favor her; the appointed time has come. . . . For the Lord will build up Zion, he will appear in his glory; he will regard the prayer of the destitute, and will not despise their supplication. Let this be recorded for a generation to come, so that a people yet unborn may praise the Lord—that he looked down from his holy height, from heaven the Lord looked at the earth to hear the groans of the prisoners, to set free those who were doomed to die; that men may declare in Zion the name of the Lord, and in Jerusalem his praise, when

> peoples gather together, and kingdoms, to worship the Lord! (Ps. 102:12-13, 16-23, NRSV).

And when the waiters did this, the very waiting itself became a prayer.

One day, Philip of Bethsaida appeared in Cana looking for his friend Nathanael—possibly at the synagogue, at his home, or just in the marketplace. Context suggests that the pair had been parted for some time but that the reunion was a welcome one. John's Gospel, in any event, tells the story with disarming brevity: "Philip found Nathanael and said to him, 'We have found him about whom Moses in the law and also the prophets wrote, Jesus son of Joseph from Nazareth'" (1:45).[9]

Nathanael, no doubt, experienced the usual thunderclap at these words; the heart that skips a beat, hope against hope—but then he regained himself. He had, of course, heard it all before. Who had Philip meant by "we"? His old fisherman friends from Capernaum, naturally—those who had gone south to Judea some while ago to become actual disciples of the Baptist.[10] Nathanael might have met them all briefly himself during his own visits to the baptism site: Andrew and Simon, sons of Jona and Joanna; and a second pair of siblings, James and John, the sons of Zebedee (a Galilean elder whose prosperous fishing enterprise had made him a respected business leader received at Herod's court). More than likely, it had been these latter two, James and John,

9 Notice that Philip does not yet seem to know about the Virgin Birth. Like the Baptist's own miraculous nativity, it was not, probably, a thing to be publicized at large but one of those facts rather, which Mary kept to herself, "pondering in her heart" (Luke 2:19).

10 Scripture here explicitly mentions Andrew; John bar Zebedee is strongly implied as another. Other members of the twelve who were present for this encounter, including Peter, may also have been John's disciples.

who started the whole thing rolling; introducing Philip and the others to the Baptist to begin with, since he was actually a kinsman of theirs—their mother Salome possibly being a cousin of his mother, Elizabeth.[11] The whole set, at any rate, would have been members of the same synagogue at Capernaum.

Nathanael's acerbic reply probably sounded more skeptical than he really intended it to be: "Can anything good come out of Nazareth?" (John 1:46). Some commentators have wondered whether this was already a proverbial expression at the time Nathanael used it; indicating both the obscurity of that tiny Galilean village to that point and an ugly reputation (borne out, perhaps, by the later story of Jesus' rejection there[12]) for being the home of an unusually ignorant and hidebound population of hicks. Given Nathanael's own humble Galilean origin, however, it seems more probable that he was only expressing perplexity at what he was being told, well-versed as he was in the biblical data that appeared to indicate some other birthplace for the coming king. Hosea, for instance, seemed to believe that God would call his son "out of Egypt," as he had once called Moses out of Pharaoh's own household (11:1); whereas it looks as if the prophet Micah meant to designate Bethlehem of Judea (a bit of an obscure backwater itself) as the favored spot—Bethlehem, which had been the birthplace of David himself, Israel's greatest king..

Nazareth, on the other hand—well, the only important figure born anywhere near Nazareth, as far as Nathanael could see, had been Jonah, who happened to be Israel's most

11 Like most genealogy, biblical or otherwise, the case for this connection is very complicated; to put it shortly, a careful comparison of the three lists of women present at the Crucifixion (Matt. 27:56, Mark 15:40, John 19:25) may identify their mother, Salome, as sister-in-law to the Blessed Virgin Mary.

12 See Matt. 13:53-58, Mark 6:1-6.

reluctant and least inspiring prophet; Jonah, who fled from God's calling at first, then groused and pouted when the people whom he pegged as targets for God's wrath actually repented at his preaching and were not destroyed, making Jonah (as he believed) look like a fool. Though it isn't actually recorded in John's brief account, Nathanael probably expressed these difficulties to his friend—and Philip probably conceded his companion's superior knowledge of Scripture. Nevertheless, Philip knew what he knew, for he had almost certainly been present in person when God made his own view on the subject known.

There was too much to explain, his heart was too full, and Philip may not have been a man of many words. So he said simply to Nathanael, "Come and see" (John 1:46).

In this case, that probably meant an afternoon's walk from Cana to Bethsaida, Philip's hometown about six miles distant. This man Jesus had, apparently, arrived there recently to enjoy the hospitality of Simon and Andrew, and ended up living under their roof for a while. The name, Nathanael had to concede, was certainly one for any Israelite to conjure with. Moses gave that exact same name to his second-in-command during the Exodus: *Yeshua*, in the Aramaic idiom, known as Joshua in English translations, but whom the Latin Bible still calls Jesus Nave.[13] Jesus the son of Nun, greatest of all the Old Testament's military saviors; Jesus whose name means, as far as we can work it out, something like "*Yahweh is salvation.*"

Jesus the son of Joseph saw Nathanael first; spotted him, like the forgiving father in his own later parable of the

13 The Latin version of the Savior's name, Jesus, was derived from the Greek transliteration *Iesous* that is actually employed in the New Testament. Western Christianity has traditionally retained that version in common usage as a method for keeping the Old and New Testament figures apart and for suggesting the unique preeminence of the latter.

prodigal, "while he was yet at a distance" (Luke 15:20). And "when Jesus saw Nathanael coming toward him, he said of him, 'Here is truly an Israelite in whom there is no deceit!'" (John 1:47).

What did Nathanael see—when he looked up for the first time into the eyes of him who the prophet Haggai called "the desire of all nations" (2:7)? As far as personal appearance goes, no one can say. Neither history nor tradition has left us any creditable description of Jesus of Nazareth's face or form. The rather dicey *Letter of Lentulus* (supposedly an eyewitness description composed by a Roman official who met him in person) depicts Jesus as "most beautiful among the children of men . . . "[14] even though Isaiah would seem to have warned us that there would be "no form or majesty . . . nothing in his appearance that we should desire him" (53:2). Lentulus writes of "hair the color of ripe hazel-nut . . . flowing over his shoulders . . . parted in two on the top of the head, after the pattern of the Nazarenes" with an abundant beard "the color of his hair, not long, but divided at the chin"—a description that happens to agree well with the image on the Shroud of Turin. Yet two of the earliest depictions in art—the *Healing of the Paralytic* found at Dura-Europos (c. 240) and the *Allegory of the Good Shepherd* located in the catacombs of Callixtus (early third century)—both show a beardless Christ. Examples like these give some sense of the difficulties involved.

Jesus has, of course, been depicted since then as a Japanese, an African, an Inuit, a white European—adopted, so to speak, into every family of man to whom his message has been carried. As long as this kind of "cultural appropriation"

14 Supposed to have been discovered in Constantinople and brought to Italy in 1421, the *Letter of Lentulus* is probably a pious fiction. One or two of its details, however, previously regarded as fabricated or anachronistic, may have been borne out by more recent scholarship.

hasn't created any unsound impression of a bodiless Christ rather than a real man, a being whose shape literally shifts to accommodate the prejudices of his hearers, there has been little harm in it. Yet the Gospels themselves do insist that Jesus was (and is!) an *Israelite*, even, in a sense, an ordinary Israelite; a Jew, descended from a long line of Jews reaching back to Judah himself, founder of that clan—though the closest the evangelists come to descriptive detail is two incidental affirmations that the shawl he wore had the traditional fringe of *tzitzit*, the specially knotted prayer tassels still worn by observant Jews today.[15]

No, what Jesus had *said* would, in Nathanaël's eyes, have been much more surprising than how he looked: "an Israelite in whom there is no deceit!'" That's probably not how Nathanael himself felt most days; a man looked upon by his peers as a diligent scholar, yet knowing himself half-hearted in prayer, feeble in faith, always second-guessing God's promises, always so ready to pronounce a harsh judgment on his elders in the schools and the Sanhedrin. Should he feel complimented at the man's rash declaration? He might have felt more tempted to do so, had not the thing been so foolish on the face of it. How on earth was this rank stranger supposed to know what his character was like? Nathanael didn't know the man from Adam, had never laid eyes on him until this very moment. How could he take such a greeting as anything but flattery?

So when he and Philip finally stood before Jesus face to face, Nathanael couldn't help protesting—and not without a hint of exasperation. He said to Jesus, "'How can you know me?'"

"When you were underneath that fig-tree," the man replied. "Before Philip called you, I saw you" (John 1:48-49).

15 These fringes are mentioned in Matthew 14:36 and Luke 8:43–44.

When the world stopped reeling, our doubtful young scribe-in-the-making found himself on his knees at Jesus' feet, clinging to the hem of his robe, crying out from his heart: "Rabbi, you are the Son of God! You are the King of Israel!" (v. 49).

Though the Gospel doesn't actually say so, we believe Jesus smiled before continuing. "Do you believe," he asked gently, "because I told you that I saw you under the fig tree? You will see greater things than these. . . . Very truly, I tell you, you will see heaven opened and the angels of God ascending and descending upon the Son of Man" (vv. 50-51).

The Messiah had gained a new apostle. And Nathanael knew what he would be doing for the rest of his life.

2
THE ROYAL FAMILY

"Wine to gladden the heart of man,
oil to make his face shine,
and bread to strengthen man's heart."

—Psalm 104:15

The very next day "there was a wedding in Cana of Galilee," Nathanael's hometown, "and the mother of Jesus was there." "Jesus and his disciples," (a pretty large group as we shall see, which included Nathanael himself by this point) "had also been invited to the wedding" (John 2:1-2). Though the names of the lucky couple aren't recorded, there are good reasons to believe that either the bride or the groom was a close relative of Mary's—a niece, nephew, or cousin, that is, of Christ himself. John the Baptist, the son of Mary's own beloved cousin Elizabeth (likely deceased), was not present; but his disciples James and John bar Zebedee undoubtedly were—both of them kinsmen, to varying degrees, of the Baptizer, his mother, and their Aunt Mary. Later, the Gospel will speak of the wedding party as having included both "his brethren and his disciples" (2:12);[16] and Nathanael would have quickly noted any overlap between those two sets.

In addition to the sons of Zebedee, a whole 'nother group of cousins or nephews or in-laws or something seemed to be enjoying hostess Mary's hospitality, too[17] (though it may well have taken the entire day for an outsider to piece the puzzle together): a second James and his brothers Judas, Joses, and Simeon, along with a group of their sisters, all grown children of another of Mary's kinsmen, Alphaeus.[18] The entire experience would, for a newcomer like Nathanael, have been exactly like being dropped into the middle of somebody else's big family reunion. He may have wondered with amusement how an outsider like himself wound up among Jesus' disciples at all, since the whole affair, it might have seemed, went largely by nepotism. It must have felt like a dream. Scarcely twenty-four hours after meeting the king of Israel for the first time, Nathanael found himself socializing

16 The Douay translation has been used here because it preserves the less specific sense of the original by employing "brethren" instead of "brothers." The Jews used the underlying Hebrew word to include many different types of kinship, not just siblings (Genesis, for instance, calls both Lot and Laban Abraham's "brothers"—when they were, more specifically, his nephew and his uncle).

17 That Mary had some kind of official role at the wedding is suggested by the way she takes responsibility for the wine shortage.

18 John 19:25 reads thusly: "But standing by the cross of Jesus were his mother, and his mother's sister, Mary the wife of Clopas, and Mary Magdalene." The parallel passages in Mark (15:40) and Matthew (27:56) would seem to identify "Mary the wife of Clopas" as the mother of James the Less and Joses. Meanwhile, "James the son of Alpheus" (who appears in all four lists of the twelve apostles) certainly seems to be identical with "James the Lord's brother" in Galatians 1:19. St. Jerome believed that Alpheus and Clopas were two names for the same man, citing the second-century chronicler Hegessipus who names a "Cleophas" as the brother of St. Joseph, husband of the blessed virgin. This identification (about which there are undoubtedly some difficulties) would make "the wife of Clopas" sister-in-law to Our Lady, with "James the son of Alpheus" and Joses her nephews by marriage.

with the entire royal family—embraced, no doubt, by strangers at regular intervals but mostly smiling dazedly in his corner, nursing a cup of wine, and trying not to say anything foolish. Yet for all its potential social discomforts, such a gathering was the ideal place at which to look a new set of companions over. Philip had become Nathanael's passkey to this new world and Philip, more than likely, made all the introductions.[19]

As we previously speculated, Andrew and Simon, James and John—the "first four" from Bethsaida—Nathanael knew already. All were, we may be certain, strong "outdoor types," displaying all of the usual virtues we associate with men who work hard for a living; but their "simplicity," we must say, has often been overstated in Sunday School accounts. All four were from *Galilee*, that region of Palestine where Israelites came into closest contact with Greco-Roman civilization and not far from the ports of Phoenicia, crossroads of the world. Andrew and Philip, in fact, are not Hebrew names at all but Greek ones, which indicates that at

19 As illustrated by the difficulties we noted above in sorting out the matter of Clopas and the three Marys, the Gospels are not as simple as we might like them to be when it comes to the familial connections between the principal players in the drama. Even such a commonplace notion as "Elizabeth was Mary's cousin" entangles us in an irritating complexity upon closer examination; the Greek text says only that Elizabeth is *suggenes*—her kinswoman, which might mean a cousin, an aunt, or some other type of female relative. The saints, at any rate, and the Fathers of the Church have spent more than 2,000 years trying to tease out the many seeming-contradictions and at-times maddening complexities involved. In this book we explore many of these fascinating genealogical theories for the sake of the fresh light they might shed on what is, for many of us, overly familiar ground. None of these conjectures, however, represents *the* answer, much less "the Church's interpretation" (since the Catholic Church has no official teaching on any of these matters beyond Christ's virginal birth from Mary, the wife of Joseph). Most recent critics, to be sure—not all of them unorthodox, by any means—have dismissed practically all such theorizing; but this author has yet to see any alternative harmonies that offer simpler answers without resulting in equal complexity.

least some of these men had roots in the larger Hellenized Jewish diaspora spread across the wide Roman Empire. Boys from this culture, whatever their class, were almost always provided with a good education at synagogue-based schools where they were taught Greek as well as Jewish wisdom. Their knowledge of the Bible, then—which they would have gleaned from the famous Greek-language version known as the Septuagint—was probably excellent *before* they came under the Baptizer's tutelage. And by the time they made the acquaintance of our scribe-in-training, it's likely that the First Four were his equals already (or nearly so) when it came to scriptural learning. All that remained was for Philip was to close the gap for his friend about how these devoted disciples of John the Baptist managed to switch their allegiance so abruptly to the unknown Nazarene instead.

Short answer? The Baptizer himself had done it, and in no uncertain terms—pronouncing his own "Mission Accomplished" and then declaring himself obsolete with the same curtness he used on those who came to offer him the crown. It happened just one day after John met Jesus for the first time—or the adult Jesus, at any rate. "[He] was standing with two of his disciples" (Andrew and probably John bar Zebedee, neither of whom appear to have been present at John's initial meeting) "and as he watched Jesus walk by he exclaimed, 'Look, here is the Lamb of God!'" (John 1:36). Hearing such a blunt, unambiguous identification from the mouth of a man who, like the rest of Israel's prophets, so often talked in symbols and allegory, must have been like a jolt from a live wire. The Nazarene, John's two disciples were told, had presented himself at the Jordan for baptism the previous afternoon—just turned up quietly in the queue along with all the other candidates, it would appear. "I myself did not know him," said John, "but I came baptizing with water for this reason, that he might be revealed to Israel" (John 1:31).

If Nathanael was at first puzzled by this statement (he had, after all, been given to understand that John and Jesus were kinsmen whose mothers, Elizabeth and Mary, had been very close) he may have later learned that the two new prophets were separated by circumstance early on. Scripture says only that the son given to Elizabeth and Zachariah "grew and became strong in spirit" and was "in the wilderness till the day of his manifestation to Israel"—not, that is, in Nazareth where Jesus grew up (Luke 1:80). Extrabiblical sources, however, may shed additional light. The *Infancy Gospel of James* (dating from about A.D. 150)[20] includes the idea that Zechariah was killed during Herod's massacre of the innocents and that his widow saved the life of the infant John by carrying him to the wild hill country between Jerusalem and the Dead Sea—where he remained until he reached the age of thirty, the standard age at which a rabbi could begin his public ministry. If this story is true, then it becomes easier to understand how the Baptizer could say "I did not know him" yet still hesitate, as he did, to baptize Jesus from a sense of unworthiness in his presence: "I need to be baptized by you, and do you come to me?" (Matt 3:14).

John's elderly mother must have lived long enough to tell her son at least some of what Mary shared about her own boy, his cousin: about how the archangel Gabriel had announced his birth, how he foretold that Jesus would be called "great" someday, "the Son of the Most High" and

20 Although the *Infancy Gospel of St. James* certainly is not Scripture and may or may not contain real traditions about the events surrounding our Lord's nativity, it is very ancient—one of the oldest Christian books in existence.

that the Lord would soon "give to him the throne of his father David . . . to reign over the house of Jacob forever" (Luke 1:32-33). Separated for so long, John may not have known his kinsman by sight but he certainly knew *of* him, knew to be on the lookout for his public debut, and to foresee, at the very least, that his own work would be complete when Jesus did finally appear. Even so, John waited for a direct confirmation from God; sensitive, perhaps, to the idea that pointing out his own cousin as Israel's new king might open him to charges of family favoritism.

And the sign was not long in coming. As he was baptizing his kinsman, John testified, "I saw the Spirit descending from heaven like a dove, and it remained on him. . . . And I myself have seen and have testified that this is the Son of God" (John 1:34). Philip, in recounting the tale, must have ended as simply as does the Gospel account: "The two disciples heard him say this, and they followed Jesus" (v. 37) Andrew quickly took the news to his brother Simon, and then Jesus himself, shortly afterward, "found Philip and said to him, 'Follow me'" (v. 43).

What had these earliest disciples of Christ learned during their apprenticeship with John the Baptist? The answer, curiously enough, may be clearer today than it has been for many generations. The Dead Sea Scrolls were discovered in caves at Qumran, just a little south of the spot where John did his baptizing; and it didn't take scholars long to notice a good many similarities between the precepts taught by the community that made the scrolls and those of the Baptizer himself. According to the Roman geographer Pliny, this area was the home of the *Essenes*, a fervent sect of monastic reformers in Judea who were highly critical of the current leadership, wished to purify Temple worship in Jerusalem (many of them may have been disaffected priests), and were intensely focused on making preparations for the imminent coming of Messiah. Like John, the Essenes spoke often of the Holy Spirit—much more so than any other Jews of that era, among whom the name is exceedingly rare. They lived an ascetic lifestyle as well: practicing celibacy, keeping only a single garment, not using money or holding any personal property. Maybe most significantly, the Essenes enjoined a ritual *baptism of repentance* on their members and linked it to Isaiah 40:3, John's favorite verse: "The voice of one crying in the desert: Prepare ye the way of the Lord, make straight in the wilderness the paths of our God" (Douay).

It would certainly explain a lot if we could really rely upon the narrative suggested by the *Infancy Gospel*—that John's father Zechariah, who had been a priest himself and was very messianically-minded, was known to the men at Qumran and sympathized with them, leaving his aged wife to turn there for help when their son's life was threatened—but such a theory remains guesswork for now. Many students of the scrolls, however, have found what seems for them to be the "smoking gun" in Qumran's celebrated *Thanksgiving Scroll*, wherein the scribes and the Pharisees are compared, at several points, to "a brood of vipers" (Matt. 3:7, Luke 3:7).

Someone like Nathanael would have had an opportunity, there at the Cana wedding, to verify the Essene influence for himself, since the First Four would have been present to fill in the blanks. Questions have been raised, for instance, by a second set of facts about the Essenes that tend to make the Baptist/Qumran connection a less-perfect fit. If Elizabeth's son really had been raised among the Essenes, he would have become a member of an intensely suspicious and inward-looking community. They showed no interest in outreach or missionary work of any kind, preferring to keep the content of their preaching a secret within their group. They tended, in fact, to despise not only the heathen *goyim* (the Gentiles and foreign outsiders) but all insufficiently worked-up Jews as well. Their whole focus was on purifying their own movement to such a degree that one of their members might one day become worthy to act as Messiah himself.

This last notion, obviously, would have been difficult for the young John to square with what he had heard from his mother about Mary's son—about Jesus of Nazareth, who was not an Essene and had no connection to Qumran—and any attempt on John's part to share this "insider information" with his superiors would probably have received a chilly reception. When his own baptizing began, John baptized all comers, believing that *all people* were being called to prepare themselves for the advent of the Savior. He is on record as having baptized tax collectors—and as having given advice to those Jewish quislings who aided the pagan occupiers and to *actual Roman soldiers* as well about how to live uprightly while continuing in their current occupations![21] Was John then, a son of Qumran who "went rogue"—who set out on his own, as several scholars have guessed, taking the sound kernel of the Essene message and refining it one step further before conveying it to a much wider audience? The First Four would have known . . . but the facts have not been preserved.

There is no doubt, however, that the message these men eventually began to preach is prefigured in the Dead Sea Scrolls: doctrines that disciples of an Essene-influenced John would probably have *carried into* their relationship with Jesus, rather than learning there. The Essenes, according to Josephus, warned of a coming Day of Judgment after which

21 See Luke 3:10-14.

the world would be burned by fire and the wicked punished eternally.[22] The *Melchizedek* document found at Qumran shows their faith in the coming of a *priest-king* who would declare a Year of Jubilee in the last days, during which God will free men from their sins and their slavery to the devil. At their noonday meal, "which was regarded apparently as a sacrificial feast, being prepared by their priests," the Essenes made an offering of bread and wine and "no stranger was admitted."[23] They taught the sweetness of martyrdom in the eyes of God and "they paid great attention to the sick, respect to the aged, and showed marked kindness and hospitality to strangers. All men were regarded as equal, and slavery was regarded as contrary to nature."[i] As Nathanael got to know his companions better, he may have begun to realize more and more that their new master was consciously building upon—even relying upon—a foundation laid by his precursor John, who really had, in a striking, unexpected way, fulfilled his prophesied mandate: "to prepare the way of the Lord, and make his paths straight."[24]

---

22 "Particularly firm is their doctrine of resurrection; they believe that the flesh will rise again and then be immortal like the soul, which, they say, when separated from the body, enters a place of fragrant air and radiant light, there to enjoy rest" (*Jewish Encyclopedia*, "Essenes," https://jewishencyclopedia.com/articles/5867-essenes).

23 "Jesus' actions at the Last Supper did not take place in a cultural vacuum. There were earlier sacred meals whose meaning and practice he was modifying. The Jewish Passover is the most obvious one" (Bergsma, *Jesus and the Dead Sea Scrolls* (New York; Image Books, 2019)). Josephus records the details of a liturgical meal shared by the Essenes which took place in a special room, required ritual ablutions beforehand along with the wearing of a white linen garment, and involved special prayers which could only be said by a priest.

24 "Also, between the ethical and the apocalyptic teachings of the Gospels and the Epistles and the teachings of the Essenes . . . the resemblance is such that the influence of the latter upon the former can scarcely be denied" (*Jewish Encyclopedia*, "Essenes").

Did the earliest disciples meet and get to know our Lord's blessed mother Mary at the wedding in Cana? This seems quite likely, since it is the first occasion on which we find all of them together in one place; and many of the facts about Jesus to which they later testify in their writings could only have come from conversations with her. Likely bearing some of the hostess duties for this affair, Mary would have been busy with many things all day long; very much the archetypical Jewish mother, she would have taken pride in every detail of the arrangements, making sure every plate was kept full, every cup stayed filled. Several of the early Fathers saw Mary here as the antitype of—the one foreshadowed by—Israel's prophetess Abigail, who arranged provisions for David's men when he and his companions were on the run from jealous King Saul.[25] The list, at any rate, of Abigail's bounty probably gives us a good record of what foods ancient Israelites might have served at a wedding: bread loaves, wine, mutton, parched grain, raisins, and yes . . . cakes of figs.[26] Recent archaeological discoveries have proved that the Jews enjoyed *beer* at such occasions as well, along with a drink less popular these days—goat milk.

Ceremonial meals were prepared by both men and women. Most scholars believe Mary's husband Joseph had died by this point, but it is quite possible that Jesus himself was pinch-hitting for him in the kitchen; there's no record, though, that our Lord did any active teaching during the festivities, having put "shop talk," it seems, on hold for the day. Busy as Mary was, however, she surely took occasional

25 Abigail earned her reputation as a prophetess by reminding David that "Yahweh will certainly make my lord a sure house, because my lord is fighting the battles of Yahweh" (1 Sam. 25:28).

26 See 1 Sam. 25:18.

breaks—and these would have been excellent times at which to become better acquainted with Jesus' growing group of "friends" (as he came to call them).

Mary was still quite young by most accounts—perhaps in her mid-forties. Her memories of the world-changing events in which she played such a central part were still fresh. As the new disciples asked their many questions, her eyes must have sparkled, her voice taken on a far-away quality. Perhaps from time to time she watched the shy young bride and groom (who may not have known each other well); possibly she was stirred by the sight to bitter-sweet recollections of the brave, loyal husband from whom she was now parted. She had "treasured" her memories for thirty years, "and pondered them in her heart" (Luke 2:19). Now perhaps, was an acceptable time to begin sharing. Jesus' birthday came just a few months after that of his cousin, the Baptist. It's very likely, then, that the two rabbis made their public debuts just those few months apart (which, in Jesus' case, had meant his baptism in the Jordan two days before the wedding) on or near their respective thirtieth birthdays. Mary may have taken this as the green light to begin a quiet ministry of her own; already "mothering" instinctively this new brood of honorary sons, ready to share family secrets.

It may have been here that Philip and Nathanael were told for the first time about Jesus' miraculous conception, his birth in a stable when there was no room at the inn, the adoration of the shepherds and of the Magi, his flight into Egypt, the way in which he had confounded the doctors at the Temple when he was only twelve. Perhaps these two cast a furtive glance sidewise from time to time as they listened, their eyes widening at the sight of Jesus nearby, helping quietly with the dinner—the chopping of vegetables or the washing of fruit. Mary's stories might, of course, already have been known to those disciples could also have been members of her extended family—to the future apostles James and John, to the less well-known James (who would come to be known one day as "the Just"), to his brothers Judas (not Iscariot) and Simon (not Peter, but Zealotes). For these, Mary's narrative and God's special mission for her son were part of a shared *blood-history*, something they had grown up with all their lives. It was the actual explanation for that "nepotism" we teased about, their special understanding of themselves as a family set apart for a mission—like Israel itself in microcosm. A special glory and a unique burden.

An early set of Church documents called the *Clementine Recognitions* asserts that the Baptizer had thirty "apostles" himself at the height of his popularity—of whom our Andrew, Simon, John (and probably James) were only the most famous.[27] It seems likely that practically all of these thirty transferred their loyalty to John's "Lamb of God" eventually, although at least some lingered with him long enough to receive the Baptizer's definitive nudge out the door: "He must increase, but I must decrease" (John 3:30). As we've already noticed, about half of those who went on to be numbered among "the twelve" were probably present at the wedding; but Jesus was inviting simply "disciples" at this stage, a much larger group of students and devotees that numbered at least seventy during the earlier phases of his ministry.[28] Hippolytus, one of the third-century Fathers, preserved what may be an authentic list of their names, and

27 Though the *Recognitions* are not reliable as history, they do contain many interesting details which may very well find their basis in fact.

28 See Luke 10:1-17.

some of these certainly could have been among those who "crashed" Mary's carefully planned wedding festivities.[ii] Included on that list are Stephen, one of the first seven deacons and the first Christian martyr; Linus, first successor to St. Peter as bishop of Rome; Ananias, who baptized St. Paul; and Paul's eventual co-workers Barnabas, Gaius, and Silas. Two of these less-famous names did compete (belatedly and under unhappy circumstances) to win the final available spot on the roster of the twelve: Joseph Bar Justus and Matthias (Matthias won). Since one of the conditions Peter had set for consideration to the post was an insistence on men who "accompanied us during all the time that the Lord Jesus went in and out among us, beginning from the baptism of John until the day when he was taken up from us"(Acts 1:21-22), it seems likely that both of these two were wedding guests as well.

This bulging guest list became a serious problem for our Lady in the end. Her son Jesus—much "given to hospitality" (a virtue enjoined upon us followers, as well, by his later servant Paul[29])—appears to have gotten a bit carried away with his invites. "The wine failed," the Gospel tells us. How could this have happened? "This was a wine country," writes Bl. Fulton Sheen, "and it is very likely that the host laid in an abundant supply. The explanation for the deficiency is probably the fact that our Blessed Lord did not come alone. He brought with him his disciples, and this apparently threw a heavy burden upon the store of wine."[iii]Mary, in her solicitude for the happiness of the young couple, seems to have noticed the wine problem before anyone else. Cups in hand were still half full, laughter continued everywhere, and so far the festivities were

29 See Rom. 12:13, 1 Tim. 3:2.

ongoing without interruption. Did she pause, hesitating at the course she was about to recommend? Scripture doesn't say so—but John bar Zebedee must have noticed a change in her demeanor and started observing her closely. His Gospel alone records the private exchange that occurred when she went to where Jesus was and approached him in a tone of intercession. Perhaps John nudged Philip or Nathanael to draw their attention to the scene, hoping to gain their help in making out what was being said.

"The mother of Jesus said to him, 'They have no wine'" (John 2:3).

This must surely have signified more than it seemed on the surface. Jesus would, no doubt, have been just as dismayed as his mother to realize that the provisions had run out. But what did she expect him to do about it—go out and buy more? Already, the disciples knew that their master was not a man of means. And even if he were financially capable, the proposed arrangements would take *time*, far too much of it: finding a merchant with enough wine on hand, arranging for the purchase, carting the large jars to the wedding site. If this was, as many scholars believe, the last day of a multi-day event (Jewish weddings often lasted five days for well-to-do families and were rarely shortened to less than three even for the poor) the climactic marriage ceremony itself would be taking place by the time the wine merchant could arrive—too late. It was easy to second Mary's emotion—but hard to know what, beyond sympathy, she wanted from her son.

Jesus' response in the next verse, however, must have been even more puzzling—as it still is for many of us: "Woman, what concern is that to you and to me? My hour has not yet come."

Rest assured that any apparent tone of shortness or

rudeness in our Lord's reply is an accidental impression created by translating a Greek form of address into English; Jesus would no more dishonor his father or mother than break any other of the Ten Commandments. And as it happens, he later used the very same Greek word translated here as "woman" when hailing the woman at the well (John 4:21), while addressing the Canaanite woman whose daughter was possessed, (Matt. 15:28), and as he spoke to the woman healed on the Sabbath (Luke 13:12)—all in situations where it is perfectly clear that no slight or diminishment is intended. Nor was Jesus belittling the importance of the problem at hand; he knew very well what was causing his mother's disquiet, shared her unhappiness over it, and confesses, even as he seems to dismiss the fact for the moment, that her concerns will always be linked to his own. Yet Jesus *was* hesitating here, as practically all of the early commentators agree. His curious answer really does seem to signify a genuine reluctance to consent to his mother's wish . . . at least for the time being. What was the holdup?

And what on earth had he meant by "his hour"?

And how could resolving Mary's wine problem possibly be connected with it?

John and the others probably decided, from the hushed way in which he and Mary spoke of it, that Jesus' "hour" must have something to do with his eventual move on Jerusalem. A new king must raise an army if he is to rise up against the old one. He must take time to gather a large enough following to guarantee success, to avoid jumping the gun as had Arthrongeus and Simon of Peraea. Yes, obviously, if Jesus were king already there would be plenty of money for wine and servants enough to move heaven and earth hauling it. So perhaps Mary was simply lamenting the fact that the whole struggle wasn't over already, that she wasn't Israel's queen mother[30] even now, so that the problem would be easy to resolve—or would never have arisen to begin with. The disciples, for instance, would certainly have remembered from their studies how David's widow Bathsheba came to King Solomon, and how the king had bowed in his mother's presence and promised to grant her whatever she wished: "Make your request, my mother; for I will not refuse you" (1 Kings 2:19-20). Jesus, they reckoned, probably wished he were in a position to give his own mother the same kind of answer—but . . . well, he said it, didn't he? "My hour has not yet come." As the prophet once wrote, "The vision awaits its appointed time; it hastens to the end—it will not lie. If it seems slow, wait for it; it will surely come; it will not delay" (Hab. 2:3). This should not be difficult to understand.

Mary *did* seem to understand—and yet persisted anyway. Her firmness suggested that she, herself, was ready to

30 Three different kinds of queens are usually recognized in an hereditary monarchy: (1) a *Queen Regnant* such as the present Elizabeth II of Britain; a queen, that is, who reigns herself, alone, without a king; (2) a *Queen Consort*, as was Isabella of Castille who sponsored the voyage of Columbus, reigning alongside her husband Ferdinand of Aragon; and (3) a *Queen Mother*, often the widow of a previous king (as was the long-lived mother of Elizabeth II, widow of George VI) who shares in the dignity of her offspring, the reigning monarch. Mary, the mother of Jesus and herself a descendant of King David, was a queen of this third type. The fact that this office existed and was recognized in the old Davidic monarchy can be seen in various passages of the books of Kings. In 1 Kings 2, David's widow Bathsheba is treated with royal dignity by his successor Solomon: "And the king rose to meet her, and bowed down to her; then he sat on his throne and had a seat brought for the king's mother; and she sat on his right. Then she said, 'I have one small request to make of you; do not refuse me.' And the king said to her, 'Make your request, my mother; for I will not refuse you'" (1 Kings 2:19-20). Most of the other kings of Judah are introduced with mention of their mothers as well; and Jehoiachin's mother, specifically, is listed (2 Kings 24:12) as part of his royal court, along with "his princes, and his palace officials." St. Elizabeth shows her awareness of this ancient usage when she greets the Blessed Virgin with the title "the mother of my Lord" (Luke 1:43).

alter the timetable, to welcome "the hour," and that she had made her peace with it in a way that even Jesus hadn't yet achieved. Perhaps a look of pain on both faces caught John and the others by surprise; a festive subject, an embarrassing but hardly earth-shattering difficulty . . . greeted by an incongruous level of solemnity. What was it the disciples might have heard earlier in the day, as Mary shared her story about the blessing of Simeon, pronounced upon both mother and son at the occasion of Jesus' presentation? "This child is destined for the falling and the rising of many in Israel, and to be a sign that will be opposed so that the inner thoughts of many will be revealed—and *a sword will pierce your own soul too*" (Luke 2:34-35). Opposition, a sign to the nation, calamity for many, and . . . Mary herself wounded to the core. The victory, in other words, would exact a toll.

Whatever the meaning, Jesus did not answer with words. The assent for which Mary was asking seems to have passed between them non-verbally—a shadow lifting from the son's features, a new peace in his eyes, an unspoken fiat. Jesus had visibly changed course. Now "the hour" that had yet to come . . . was already here. So be it. Mary turned to the servants and said very simply, "Do whatever he tells you."

The actual miracle happened backstage, so to speak:

> Now standing there were six stone water jars for the Jewish rites of purification, each holding twenty or thirty gallons. Jesus said to the servants, "Fill the jars with water. And they filled them up to the brim. And he said to them, "Now draw some out and take it to the chief steward. So they took it. When the steward tasted the water that had become wine, and did not know where it came from (though the servants who had drawn the water knew), the steward called the

> bridegroom and said to him, "Everyone serves the good wine first, and then the inferior wine after the guests have become drunk. But you have kept the good wine until now" (John 2:6-10).

For a miracle often interpreted as a sign to the nation—the starting gun, as it were, for Christ's whole ministry of miracles—the quietness of the thing has been too-little commented upon. St. John Chrysostom, in one of his fourth century homilies on John's Gospel, provides helpful analysis:

> If lowly servants had related what happened they would have been thought mad in testifying to something that was done by someone who at the time appeared to be a mere man. Although they knew for certain what they had experienced . . . yet that would have been insufficient to convince anyone else. And so Jesus did not reveal it to everyone but to the one who was best able to understand what had happened, [to the wine steward, that is] reserving a clearer understanding for a later time. . . . Although the miracle was not revealed right at that moment, yet in the end it could not be passed by in silence since so many and such convincing testimonies had been provided by Christ for the future.[iv]

Knowing that word was sure to get out, Jesus realized very well that the miracle would *become* a sign . . . but that doesn't seem to have been the main point. Even the apostles, after all, are left at this stage to take the word of the kitchen help. Why, then, *did* he do it? Sometimes the best explanation of a text lies right on the surface: Jesus changed the water into wine . . . because his mother asked him to.

Hindsight can be blinding. St. Maximus of Turin (who wrote early in the fifth century) believed that the miracle at Cana was sufficient proof that Jesus of Nazareth is God incarnate: "This transformation of the water from its own substance into another testified to the powerful presence of the Creator. Only he who made it out of nothing could change water into something whose use was quite different. Dearly beloved, have no doubt that he who changed water into wine is the same as he who from the beginning thickened it into snow and hardened it into ice . . . he who changed it into blood for the Egyptians and bade it flow from the dry rock for the thirsty Hebrews."[v] Maximus is, of course, not incorrect here, but this is an argument that proves too much. Elijah the prophet, after all, performed a similar wonder in his era—keeping a jug of oil and a pot of meal miraculously full for many days to save the widow of Zarephath—without actually being God himself.[31] So the Cana miracle alone would not have driven witnesses to the full truth about the Nazarene. Yet just the realization that their new master was fully the equal of Elijah—whom the Israelites universally regarded as "loftiest and most wonderful of the prophets"[vi]—in power and in favor with God would have been quite enough to dazzle his disciples at this stage. This realization alone would have been enough to convince the future apostles that they had hitched their wagons to the proper star, Messiah-wise—but wouldn't yet have disclosed the fact that they were, by doing so, getting a great deal more than they bargained for.

We twenty-first-century readers, of course, know to expect a miracle from the moment we put the words *Cana* and *wedding* together. Every Catholic who has sat through Mass knows that we confess Jesus as "God from God, light

31 See 1 Kings 17:8-16.

from light, true God from true God, begotten, not made, consubstantial with the Father." But like the math student who is allowed to give the correct answer without showing his work, we modern Christians too often regurgitate a good enough response without really understanding how we got there. Jesus' earliest disciples, though, had no such advantage. Any bare declarations at this stage that "this man Jesus is God" (which the Gospels wholly deny us) would have caused a mental and spiritual short circuit. His new disciples simply couldn't have processed such a phrase in any profitable way. Had not Moses written, "God is not a man, that he should lie, nor as the Son of Man, that he should be changed" (Num. 23:19)? Christ's pupils would have to be led along by degrees. This is why the great Chrysostom prefaced his remarks from a moment ago with these words: "Our Lord wanted the power of his miracles to be seen gradually, little by little." Why? Because they could not really be "seen" any other way.

As we have noticed already, all of the prophetic titles the disciples had heard so far could be taken in a less fundamentally astounding sense (and were so taken by perfectly orthodox, faith-filled Hebrew scholars of the day). Even Mary's message of a virgin birth was not, of itself, a sign of her son's divinity: God has quite enough power to cause a more ordinary man to be virgin-born without making him, *ipso facto*, into the incarnation of the Second Person of the Trinity. Jesus' disciples—and especially those who would soon come to be singled out as "the twelve"—were being called to make that journey themselves. There were questions to ask first, many of them stupid. There were blind alleys to discover. And the finding of these questions was, as in many more mundane inquiries as well, the indispensable prerequisite to finding the answers.

Nevertheless, John the Evangelist finishes his Gospel

account of the wedding with these words: "Jesus did this, the first of his signs, in Cana of Galilee, and revealed his glory; and his disciples believed in him" (2:11). Even here, at the very start of their journey, the disciples show forth their little "mustard seed" of faith . . . and thus merit further revelations. Yet this would have been a verse that Nathanael, at least, knew not to take *quite* literally—for even without their long training under the Baptizer he had gained a leg up on his new compadres when it came to belief. Cana may have been the first *public* miracle, but, just the day before, Nathanael had seen a quiet wonder of his own.

3

MIRACLE MEN

"When the crowds found out about [the miracles]
they followed him; and he welcomed them,
and spoke to them about the kingdom of God,
and healed those who needed to be cured."

—Luke 9:11

Before he did any teaching at all, he did miracles.

Scholars who have worked to create a "harmony of the Gospels" through the centuries (the earliest known attempt was Tatian's *Diatessaron* around A.D. 150) have noticed something odd and not widely recognized about the very beginning of Christ's life with the apostles. Jesus, it would appear, gathered most of them up, showed them something uncanny at Cana to retain their interest . . . and then left Galilee abruptly on an out-of-town trip. For reasons of his own, he made a brief journey to the holy city during Passover, a pilgrimage to which the "First Four plus two" (Philip and Nathanael) do not seem to have been invited. Andrew and Simon, James and John, at least, apparently wandered back to their day jobs for the time being, awaiting their more famous call (Matt. 4:18-22, Mark 1:16-20) to leave their nets behind for good and become full-time "fishers of men." And Jesus, having not yet begun to disciple his ostensible disciples, did little to no teaching during his sojourn in the south.[32]

One can't help wondering if his followers puzzled over this kind of treatment while he was away—perhaps even grumbled, as the Israelites did when Moses lingered on the mountain. What was Jesus up to down there in Jerusalem? Sizing up his support among the Jews?[33] Recruiting Judean disciples to add to his existing band of Galileans? (Practically all of Jesus' followers were northern natives so far; and, indeed, only one single Judean ever was numbered among the twelve.) Perhaps he was scouting out the lay of the land for future military action? Whatever it was, it was apparently "Messiah business," and far above the pay grade of those left behind.

These early disciples, it must be noted, were relying heavily, indeed almost exclusively, on the word of the Baptizer up to this point . . . and they may have decided that the two cousins compared poorly so far. John had not treated them like this, perhaps; and switching over to the Nazarene,

32 What little he did was parenthetical to his interactions with two persons entirely outside the circle of disciples (at least to begin with): Nicodemus (John 3) and the Samaritan woman (John 4). This unnamed woman, incidentally, became the recipient of Jesus' one and only direct affirmation of the title so many were wondering about: "The woman said to him, 'I know that Messiah is coming' (who is called Christ). 'When he comes, he will proclaim all things to us.' Jesus said to her, 'I am he, the one who is speaking to you'" (John 4:25-26).

33 By this time, "the Jews" was often used as a geographic rather than a religious term. The once-unified nation of the Israelites had been divided during the disastrous reign of Rehoboam into the northern confederacy of Israel proper (later, the Samaritans) and the southern kingdom of Judah. It was residents of this southern kingdom who were called Jews at the time of Christ (and specially, of the region around Jerusalem) in contradistinction to both the Samaritans and the religiously orthodox but ethnically diverse Galileans of northern Judah.

quiet thus far and inscrutable, may have been confusing at first, even disappointing. And if, as seems to be the case, the breaking news of John's imprisonment by Herod (brought on by the Baptizer's "meddling" in the private lives of the royal household) arrived during this same period of Jesus' absence, then the sense of loss and of nostalgia for their previous mentor would have been exaggerated to an even more acute degree.

When he did return to Galilee, Jesus went straight to the synagogues where, as a recognized rabbi, he was entitled to preach. As he did so, he was "praised by everyone" (Luke 4:15)—or almost everyone, since members of his own home synagogue at Nazareth, having heard his negative assessment of the state of their faith, had become incensed and driven him off the property. But he likely gave the same short presentation at each of the synagogues he visited. The one described in Luke 4:16-21 may be taken as typical: "He stood up to read, and the scroll of the prophet Isaiah was given to him. He unrolled the scroll and found the place where it was written: 'The Spirit of the Lord is upon me, because he has anointed me to bring good news to the poor. He has sent me to proclaim release to the captives and recovery of sight to the blind, to let the oppressed go free, to proclaim the year of the Lord's favor.' And he rolled up the scroll, gave it back to the attendant, and sat down."

These readings were, of course, universally recognized as a prophecy of the long-expected Deliverer to come. For Essenes, however, and those familiar with their ideas, the choice of this particular reading would have been doubly dramatic. Qumran's Melchizedek Scroll, recall, ties this passage from Isaiah directly to Essene expectations of a great jubilee, a day when the Messiah would liberate mankind, "releasing them from the debt of all their sins," and "deliver them from the power of Belial,[34] and from the power of all the spirits predestined to him."[vii] Either way, as Luke continues, "the eyes of all in the synagogue were fixed on him." Jesus seems to have allowed the words of the reading to hang on the air a moment or two, "then he began to say to them, 'Today this scripture has been fulfilled in your hearing'" (Luke 4:21). *Israel's great prophet*, in other words . . . *was writing about me.*

As we've already noted, self-proclaimed messiahs had come and gone before this one, so we needn't jump directly to the conclusion that all the Galileans who heard this announcement were, like those at Nazareth, deficient somehow in their faith. Those who took a "wait and see" approach were actually behaving properly: "Do not believe every spirit," as St. John later wrote, "but test the spirits to see whether they are of God; for many false prophets have gone out into the world" (1 John 4:1). Promises had been made about this event, after all; sacred words that Israelites had been learning by heart for the last fifteen centuries. And, as Jesus said himself in a later context, "Everything written about me in the law of Moses, the prophets, and the psalms must be fulfilled (Luke 24:44). The proof of the pudding would be in the eating. "Wisdom is vindicated by her deeds" (Matt. 11:19).

Jesus accepted the challenge. "He went down to Capernaum," probably the very next week, "and was teaching them on the Sabbath. . . . In the synagogue there was a man who had the spirit of an unclean demon," and clearly,

34 "Found frequently as a personal name in the Vulgate and various English translations of the Bible, [Belial] is commonly used as a synonym of Satan. This sense is derived from 2 Corinthians 6:15, where Belial (or Beliar) as prince of darkness is contrasted with Christ, the light. It is clear in the Vulgate and Douay translations of 1 Kings 21:10 and 13, where the same Hebrew is rendered once as Belial and twice as 'the devil'" (*Catholic Encyclopedia*, "Belial," https://www.newadvent.org/cathen/02408a.htm).

since that man had the demon there with him "in the synagogue," the existing religious authorities had been powerless to help. The possessed man

> cried out with a loud voice, "Let us alone! What have you to do with us, Jesus of Nazareth? Have you come to destroy us? I know who you are, the Holy One of God." But Jesus rebuked him, saying, "Be silent, and come out of him!" When the demon had thrown him down before them, he came out of him without having done him any harm. They were all amazed and kept saying to one another, "What kind of utterance is this? For with authority and power he commands the unclean spirits, and out they come!" (Luke 4:33-36).

Next, he went to Simon's house—Simon who, along with at least some of the others, must have been eyewitness to both the announcement and the accompanying exorcism. "Now Simon's mother-in-law was suffering from a high fever, and they asked [Jesus] about her. Then he stood over her and rebuked the fever, and it left her. Immediately she got up and began to serve them" (Luke 4:39).

"As the sun was setting"—still on the same Sabbath day, mind you—"all those who had any who were sick with various kinds of diseases brought them to him; and he laid his hands on each of them and cured them. Demons also came out of many, shouting, 'You are the Son of God!' But he rebuked them and would not allow them to speak, because they knew that he was the Messiah" (Luke 4:40-41). This affirmation expressed a certainty that the apostles, along with the rest of humanity, had not yet *earned*—but the lesson, as you can believe, was now well under way.

The next day, a Sunday, Jesus left to go south again—another fifty-mile walk or more. "I must proclaim the good news of the kingdom of God to the other cities also; for I was sent for this purpose'—and do notice that "proclaiming the good news" at this stage chiefly meant laying claim to ancient prophecies and then making good on the claims. "So he continued proclaiming the message in the synagogues of Judea" (Luke 4:43-44). He healed a leper along the way, and "many crowds would gather to hear him and to be cured of their diseases" (Luke 5:15).

A group of men brought a paralytic and tried to lay him before Jesus, "but finding no way to bring him in because of the crowd, they went up on the roof and let him down with his bed through the tiles into the middle of the crowd in front of Jesus. When he saw their faith, he said, 'Friend, your sins are forgiven you.' Then the scribes and the Pharisees began to question, 'Who is this who is speaking blasphemies? Who can forgive sins but God alone?'" (Luke 5:17-24).

Jesus saw where these rhetorical questions were going, and answered, "Why do you raise such questions in your hearts? Which is easier to say, 'Your sins are forgiven you,' or to say, 'Stand up and walk'? But so that you may know that the Son of Man has authority on earth to forgive sins'—he said to the one who was paralyzed—'I say to you, stand up and take your bed and go to your home.'" The man stood up, and went home, "glorifying God." The assembled group, "filled with awe," likewise glorified God, saying, "We have seen strange things today" (Luke 5:25-27).

Strange things, yes; but what these witnesses had seen was nothing more or less than the same old signs their prophets always told them to expect. Were the men of Qumran looking for a new Melchizedek who could deliver humanity from the power of Belial? Jesus rebukes devils and out they go. Were the Essenes expecting a priest-king to begin releasing men from the debt of their sins? The Nazarene says, "Your sins are forgiven" and the sinner is healed as proof of a successful transaction. Isaiah had promised recovery of sight to the blind and (that the ears of the deaf would be unstopped, the lame made to leap like deer (35:5-6, 42:6-7)—a miracle-worker, in other words. And now here Jesus was, working the promised miracles.

In later chapters, our Lord himself affirms this interpretation. Asked for proof that the Baptizer's identification had been correct when he named him "Lamb of God," Jesus provides the following "you tell me" response: go, he says, and report simply that "the blind receive their sight, the lame walk, the lepers are cleansed, the deaf hear, the dead are raised, and the poor have good news brought to them" (Matt. 11:2-4). Accused by the rabbis of performing his signs through the power of black magic, Jesus reminds them that demons don't drive out demons and leads them to the conclusion, "If it is by the finger of God that I cast out the demons, then the kingdom of God has come to you" (Luke 11:19-20). Jesus' wonders, thus, are not only a valid but an *essential* stamp of God's approval on his mission. Unbiased spectators saw this very well, even as the religious authorities offered compelling theological arguments against the Nazarene's claim: "Yet many in the crowd believed in him and were saying, 'When the Messiah comes, will he do more signs than this man has done?'" (John 7:31).

For the disciples, all of this must have happened awfully fast. Before his teaching began in earnest with the Sermon on the Mount, before they even got to know him at all, with hardly a word of explanation from the man himself the future apostles watched dozens and dozens of signs and wonders take place at the Nazarene's command:

"They brought to him all the sick, those who were afflicted with various diseases and pains, demoniacs, epileptics, and paralytics, and he cured them" (Matt. 4:24);

"Whenever the unclean spirits saw him, they fell down before him and shouted, 'You are the Son of God!'" (Mark 3:11); and

"They brought to him all who were sick or possessed with demons. And the whole city was gathered around the door" (Mark 1:32-33).

It is important to realize that these early chapters of the four Gospels contain a truly unprecedented outpouring of the miraculous. Many who haven't yet studied the Bible carefully harbor an impression that Scripture is chock-a-block with signs and wonders—a miracle on practically every page. This isn't the case at all. During certain phases of Israel's history, centuries go by with scarcely a whiff of the supernatural. Even when Moses began to lead the people "there had been no appearance of Jehovah to any one for above four hundred years, and they might well think that the age of miracles was past," according to the great Anglican scholar Charles Ellicott. "Miracles cluster around certain crises in God's dealings with man," Ellicott continues, often "ceasing altogether between one crisis and another."[viii] In fact, the whole 500 years before Christ's great Galilee ministry began—since the days when Daniel had been delivered from the lion's den—had been one of these dry periods.

If we distinguish between miracles worked directly by God at his own initiative and those "called down" in some manner by a human wonder-worker—an audible plea, for instance, or the use of some sacramental medium like Moses' rod of power or the salt with which Elisha healed the poisonous waters of Jericho—then miracles of the type worked by Jesus are rare indeed in the Old Testament. Moses did twelve or fifteen, depending on how many of the Egyptian plagues we reckon were commenced at his word (and at least one of those was actually performed by his brother Aaron using Moses' rod). Joshua worked about four such miracles during his career and Elijah and Elisha about twelve each.

Jesus of Nazareth, on the other hand, may well have performed *twelve an hour* some days. Nearly forty, at any rate, are individually described in the Gospels, but the actual total is impossible to calculate. They came in such a flood that large numbers of them are often lumped together in indefinite masses, as Luke relates: "He came down with them and stood on a level place, with a great crowd of his disciples and a great multitude of people from all Judea, Jerusalem, and the coast of Tyre and Sidon. They had come to hear him and to be healed of their diseases. . . . And all in the crowd were trying to touch him, for power came out from him and healed all of them" (Luke 6:19). This is but one of fifteen or so similar passages.

So when our Lord did finally begin to teach his disciples, we may be sure that he had their full attention. In their eyes, he was no longer auditioning for the part; they had ceased comparing him to the Baptist or, indeed, to any other prophet. The eruption of miracles had simply blown all quibbles away. They still entertained, to be sure, half-a-dozen contradictory ideas about the role he had come to play, but now they considered the puzzle from a new position: sitting at his feet—figuratively and then often literally speaking.

Again, we mustn't allow hindsight to blind us to the real difficulty of their task. Here was a lineal descendant of King David and thus legitimately in line for the throne—but with astonishing powers David never dreamed of; surely there was no longer any doubt that the Nazarene would himself be king of the Jews someday soon. But what *kind* of a king?

David, so symbolic of Christ in other ways, had been primarily a man of war. He had so much blood on his hands, in fact, that when he conceived his plan to build the first great Temple at Jerusalem God forbade it: "You shall not build a house to my name, because you have shed so much blood before me upon the earth" (1 Chron. 22:8). To build his Temple, God wanted a man of peace, to better signal his intention for it to be "a house of prayer for all peoples" where "the foreigners who join themselves to the Lord" could be gathered one day, "to minister to him, to love the name of the Lord, and to be his servants" (Isa. 56:6-7). So David's son Solomon (whose name is based on the Hebrew word for peace) built the Temple instead; and his reign really was notable for peace with all the surrounding nations.

Comparisons between King Solomon and King Jesus, however, seemed strained in other ways. So far from being, like the Nazarene, a chaste and humble man ready to identify with the poor, Solomon was famous for the luxury and sensuousness of his lifestyle, living in a palace of untold riches with his dozens of wives and perhaps hundreds of concubines. A handful of the other Israelite kings had been good men, it's true, but none of these were particularly characterized by compassion for the suffering either—and certainly none of them had done miracles. To put the point simply, the apostles really had no pre-existing category in which to file a king destined to break the rod of the oppressor "as in the days of Midian" . . . who also works wonders of healing and tenderness like Elijah or Elisha.

This is why "the kingdom of God"—kingship, that is, in the hands of a man who is God's own Son—immediately became the central focus of Jesus' discipleship program. His miracles showed that "the kingdom of God has come to you." Now, his followers will learn what that term (for which Matthew's Gospel substitutes "kingdom of heaven" as a way to avoid using the sacred name of God with his Jewish target readership) will mean in the mouth of their new king. In this sense, the phrase did not admit of a short, direct Webster-style definition, nor does it today; Jesus, in fact, would spend the next two and a half years or so saying things like:

"With what can we compare the kingdom of God, or what parable shall we use for it?" (Mark 4:30);

"The kingdom of heaven is like treasure hidden in a field" (Matt. 13:44);

"The kingdom of heaven may be compared to a king who gave a marriage feast for his son" (Matt. 22:2); and

"The kingdom of God is not coming with signs to be observed; nor will they say, 'Lo, here it is!' or 'There!' for behold, the kingdom of God is in the midst of you" (Luke 17:20-21).

In much the same way that Jesus was slowly revealing the fullness of his own identity to his men, so his pupils would, apparently, have to *live through* the learning of this great expression. No one could simply be told, not at least without danger of grave misunderstanding.

This did not mean, however, that certain definite propositions couldn't be gathered along the way. Though the kingdom, for instance, had already "come to" God's chosen people with the arrival of Christ, Jesus nevertheless teaches his disciples to pray that it *will* come (as in the Lord's Prayer) and then promises that some of them "will not taste death before they see the kingdom of God come with power (Mark 9:1). With a little meditation, these things seemed to imply a *complete package* that has, in some sense, already been delivered but which must, even so, still be "unboxed" somehow as long as it exists . . . with well-recognized indicators of progress along the way. This conception was then reinforced by a whole series of rather elusive parables about small beginnings and hidden greatness only gradually uncovered: a pearl of great price, the presence of which not everyone has yet realized; a tiny, almost invisible mustard seed from which a great tree must eventually spring; a small bit of leaven that slowly transforms the whole lump of dough.

At other times, Jesus seemed to identify his kingdom with "the bosom of Abraham"—the abode of the saints after death, that is. "I tell you," he said, that "many will come from east and west and sit at table with Abraham, Isaac, and Jacob in the kingdom of heaven" (Matt. 8:11) but "unless one is born anew, he cannot see the kingdom of God" (John 3:3). But then elsewhere in his talk, it becomes clear that membership in the kingdom of God is, in Jesus' eyes, not to be simply identified with final blessedness or even election to salvation; he compares it to a net containing both good and bad fish, to a field containing both wheat and tares, to a wedding party made up of both wise and foolish virgins. The bad fish are thrown away, the tares are burned, and the foolish virgins are shut out—yet all were once part of "the kingdom." So the kingdom, as his disciples slowly began to glean, would *flower* finally in the abode of the blessed . . . but the flower has its roots in the earth.

And then, just as his disciples were beginning to grasp some of this, Jesus did something totally new and dramatic, something often overlooked today, which made the plan clearer to his contemporaries than any mere words could have. Luke's Gospel tells it this way: "Now during those days he went out to the mountain to pray; and he spent the night in prayer to God." The time had come for our Lord to make a decision about a matter weighty enough, it would seem, to require an unusually lengthy vigil . . . even for the Lord's Christ. "And when day was come, he called unto him his disciples; and he chose twelve of them (whom also he named apostles): Simon, whom he [later] surnamed

Peter, and Andrew his brother, James and John [the sons of Zebedee], Philip and Bartholomew [*Bar Tolomais*, that is, our own Nathanael], Matthew and Thomas, James the son of Alpheus, and Simon who is called Zelotes, and Jude, the brother of James, and Judas Iscariot, who was the traitor" (Luke 6:12-16 (Douay). These twelve, for whom magnificent churches and mighty cities have been named all over the earth, are now universally known as "the twelve apostles."

We might wonder immediately, "What was the distinction between a *disciple* and an *apostle*?" The word itself doesn't give us much help, since *apostolos*, in Greek, means simply "one who has been sent out"—entrusted with a mission. And yet the remaining disciples, those from among whom the twelve had been selected, were not dismissed after the choice was made but continued rather to be trained by their master and were eventually (as we will see a little later) "sent out" by him on what would appear to be the exact same mission.[35]

Some commentators have noticed that what is almost surely the underlying Aramaic word here—*slikha*—had a much more specific meaning than *apostolos*. According to

35 In the Gospels, "the name apostle denotes principally one of the twelve disciples who, on a solemn occasion, were called by Christ to a special mission . . . But in other books of the New Testament, chiefly in the Epistles of St. Paul and in the Acts, this use of the word is current. Saul of Tarsus, being miraculously converted, and called to preach the Gospel to the heathens, claimed with much insistency this title and its rights . . . The word apostle has also in the New Testament a larger meaning, and denotes some inferior disciples who, under the direction of the apostles, preached the Gospel, or contributed to its diffusion; thus Barnabas (Acts 14:4, 14), probably Andronicus and Junias (Rom. 16:7), Epaphroditus (Phil. 2:25), two unknown Christians who were delegated for the collection in Corinth (2 Cor. 8:23). We know not why the honorable name of apostle is not given to such illustrious missionaries as Timothy, Titus, and others who would equally merit it" (*Catholic Encyclopedia*, "Apostles," https://www.newadvent.org/cathen/01626c.htm).

the nineteenth-century English theologian J.B. Lightfoot, early Jews used this word (*seliah* in Hebrew form) as a term for "those who were dispatched from the mother city by the rulers of the race on any foreign mission, especially such as were charged with collecting the tribute paid to the temple service."[ix] In this sense, "apostle" might imply someone called to a *diplomatic* mission: men who have been specially credentialed, that is, above and beyond more ordinary officials, to be envoys or legates carrying a delegated authority to resolve disputed claims or otherwise conduct business on behalf of their sovereign.

Be that as it may, the word *apostolos* is actually less important in Gospel usage than another more frequently employed term: *dodeka*—the twelve. St. Mark says that Jesus "appointed the twelve" (3:14), "called the twelve" (6:7), "took the twelve aside" (10:32); Luke says, "the twelve were with him" (8:1) and that he "called the twelve together." Matthew's Gospel might really throw us a curve if we didn't realize that *dodeka* had become a coined expression by the time that sacred book came to be written, for there the author feels free to completely interchange the two original terms!—"His twelve disciples" (11:1), "These are the names of the twelve apostles" (10:2), and "He took the twelve disciples aside by themselves" (20:17).

What was the dramatic signal sent by this act of choosing twelve—and only twelve—such legates? Simply put, *the number itself* represented a claim to messianic kingship. Amos (one of Israel's "twelve prophets," by the way[36]) had

36 In the Hebrew Bible, the individual works we Christians usually designate as the *minor prophets* (a term that originated with St. Augustine) are grouped together in a single book known as "The Twelve Prophets" or often just "The Twelve." In Christian Bibles, they appear as twelve individual Old Testament books: Hosea, Joel, Amos, Obadiah, Jonah, Micah, Nahum, Habakkuk, Zephaniah, Haggai, Zechariah, and Malachi.

foreseen, some 700 years previously, a coming time of restoration once the nation's long period of foreign captivity had run its course: "In that day will I raise up the tabernacle of David that is fallen, and close up the breaches thereof; and I will raise up his ruins, and I will build it as in the days of old" (Amos 9:1, KJV (see also Acts 15:16)). For Essenes, especially, this "fallen tabernacle" had been the one, united Israelite kingdom that flourished under David and Solomon, home not only of the Jews descended from Judah but of the other eleven tribes as well, sired by Reuben, Zebulon, Naphtali and the rest of the Hebrew patriarchs.[37] Yet even for non-Essenes this lost unity was widely seen as the underlying cause of the nation's enfeebled and prostrate condition, of her humiliating subjugation to the heathen Romans.

As a result, the fulfilling of Amos's prophecy was very high on their "to do" list for any prospective Messiah (far too high, as we shall see, with "freeing the people from their slavery to Belial" a distant second at best). Another widely believed end-times prophecy of the day, circulating in a relatively recent (c. 100 B.C.) Jewish apocalypse called *The Testament of the Twelve Patriarchs,* presents the patriarch Benjamin, youngest of Jacob's twelve sons, foreseeing a future "resurrection" both for himself and for his eleven brethren: "Then shall we also rise, each one over our tribe, worshipping the king of heaven."[x] With all eyes turned his way now, thanks to the veritable tsunami of miracles, Jesus' gathering and training of a large group of disciples had become well known. Many observers must have remembered

37 The Qumranites, in fact, never called themselves "Jews," even though they did actually reside in Judea; they spoke of themselves instead as "sons of Israel" and prayed every day for the restoration prophesied by Amos. Jesus himself generally sticks to these same terms, saying "Israel" or "the children of Israel"—all twelve tribes, in other words—rather than "Jews" as a description of the people he has come to save.

that David's first successor had picked twelve royal officers as well, as recorded in 1 Kings 4:7-8. Now, with the elevation of twelve *slikha* specially deputized to act in his name, the nation realized suddenly what this new claimant to David's crown was training his men *for.*

Later, in a passage we will examine much more carefully, Jesus astonished the twelve themselves with a prophecy of his own: "Truly I tell you, at the renewal of all things, when the Son of Man is seated on the throne of his glory, you who have followed me will also sit on twelve thrones, judging the twelve tribes of Israel" (Matt. 19:28). What on earth, as many (both Christians and skeptics) have asked since then, can a group of lowly fishermen have done to get their names engraved on the pillars of heaven? They seem to have been pleasant chaps, to be sure—though caught, we must confess, just once or twice too often asking a foolish question or speaking out of turn. But doesn't writing about them, as St. Paul will eventually do, as the foundation (along with the Old Testament prophets) of "the household of God" (1 Tim. 2:19-20) . . . isn't that getting just a little carried away?

The answer—or the *beginning* of an answer, at any rate—becomes apparent during Matthew's account of their original call: "Jesus summoned his twelve disciples and gave them authority over unclean spirits, to cast them out, and to cure every disease and every sickness (Matt. 10:1). With one stroke, in other words, the lowly fishermen weren't so lowly anymore (not, at least, in any sense that wouldn't also be appropriate for describing their Lord himself). The one unique Miracle Man . . . has suddenly become thirteen. If Jesus regards his own miracles as evidence of special unction from God—and he does: "Believe me that I am in the Father and the Father is in me; but if you do not, then believe me because of the works themselves" (John 14:10-11)—then these twelve delegates have also received

God's stamp of approval. "[They] went out," Mark testifies, "and proclaimed the good news everywhere, while the Lord worked with them and confirmed the message by the signs that accompanied it" (Mark 16-20). Most astonishing of all: by the end of our story, any single one of these lowly fishermen would, because of this gift, rank high on the list of all-time Bible wonder-workers; well ahead, like Jesus himself, of Joshua or Elijah or even Moses.

St. Cyril of Alexandria, that great fifth-century Father and Doctor, saw the twelve apostles prefigured, along with their master, in another of the great prophet's phrases: "Blessed Isaiah says of him and the holy apostles, 'Behold, a just king shall reign, and princes shall rule with judgment' [Isa 32:1]."[xi] Here, Cyril may have had in mind the twelve stones on the "Breastplate of Judgment"—the sacred *khosen,* worn by the high priest of Israel, containing the *Urim* and *Thummim* that Aaron and his successors had consulted in order to determine God's will in certain situations. And each stone on the breastplate bore the name of one of the twelve patriarchs—the first group of men, that is, to have sat on "twelve thrones judging the twelve tribes of Israel."

Good rule of thumb for future reference? Numbers in the Bible (especially the number twelve) are almost never a coincidence.

Another of the early Fathers, St. Jerome, points out one more important consideration—and not without an ironic hint of tragedy for the pages to come:

> The kind and merciful Lord and master does not begrudge his followers and disciples their powers. Even as he had healed every disease and every infirmity, he empowered his apostles to heal every disease and infirmity. But there is a great gap between having and granting, between

giving and receiving. Whatever he does, he does in the power of the Lord. Whatever they do, they display their own weakness and the power of the Lord, saying, "In the name of Jesus, arise and walk." It must be noted, further, that the power to work miracles is granted to the apostles even to the twelfth man.[xii]

4

THE OBSCURITIES OF PARABLES

He who devotes himself to the study of the law of the Most High . . . will be concerned with prophecies . . . and penetrate the subtleties of parables; he will seek out the hidden meanings of proverbs and be at home with the obscurities of parables.

—Sirach 39:1-3

Early in his exploration of the writings left by the Church Fathers, Anglican presbyter John Henry Newman (now St. John Henry Newman) discovered that the primitive Church approached evangelization and Christian initiation in a completely different way than we do.[38]

Rather than beginning with the Divinity of Christ, the blood atonement offered on the cross, or the holy Trinity as

38 This and all quotations from St. John Henry Newman in this chapter are taken from *The Arians of the Fourth Century* (Notre Dame, IN: University of Notre Dame Press, 2001), Sect. III. All citations from the early Fathers in this chapter are Newman's own original translations prepared for use within that book.

similar classes for new Christians have done so often since, Newman saw that the early Church had a settled practice of holding her profoundest doctrines in reserve, keeping them deliberately away from inquirers and catechumens, actually saving them as secrets, in fact, until much later in the process of formation. "These things must not be told to the uninitiated," wrote St. Basil during a discourse on the Divinity of the Holy Spirit, "One must not circulate in writing the doctrine of mysteries which none but the initiated are allowed to see."

St. Cyril, bishop of Jerusalem, writing instructions for one of his catechists, warned thusly: "Tell nothing to a stranger; for we deliver a mystery . . . You, yourself, were once a catechumen . . . and while you were, I did not tell you what was coming." "We speak in obscure terms concerning the Divine Mysteries," explained the historian Theodoret, "on account of the uninitiated, but when they have withdrawn we teach the initiated plainly."

Newman saw the principle being lived out to a startling degree. The Lord's Prayer, for instance, was not disclosed to catechumens until just before baptism. St. Ambrose told his sister in a letter that he'd been teaching the Creed to those of the newly baptized who were "sufficiently advanced." One particular quote from St. Augustine made the day-to-day reality of the thing about as vivid as possible: "If you say to a catechumen, 'Do you believe in Christ?' he will answer, 'I do,' and will sign himself with the cross . . . But if you ask him, 'Do you eat the flesh and drink the Blood of the Son of Man?' he will not know what you mean, for Jesus has not yet trusted himself to him."

Previous scholars had called it the *Disciplina Arcana*, the "discipline of the secret." They guessed that it was enforced because of the Church's underground position at the time—to guard against the danger of admitting a Trojan Horse into the community during periods of persecution. Newman, however, discerned some problems with that thesis. All of the quotes presented above, for instance, date from seventy-five to a hundred years *after* Christianity had been legalized by Constantine. The early Church's "rule of reticence," therefore, remained in effect long after persecution had ceased. Newman also noticed that no early writer ever explained the regimen in terms of confidentiality. Whenever they did address themselves to the question of why such methods were employed, the Fathers instead emphasized the unfitness of uninitiated persons to profitably hear them. St. Clement of Alexandria says he withheld the deeper truths from his pupils "because the ear that hears does not yet deserve to receive it." Sts. John Chrysostom, Gregory Nazianzus, and Cyril of Jerusalem all cite the inability of new converts to understand Christian theology prior to gaining the sacramental light of baptism.

Interesting facts, to be sure—but why bring this up now, in a story about the call of Christ's twelve apostles?

Well, Newman himself reached the conclusion that this ancient practice constituted nothing more or less than a pattern that those apostles learned from Jesus personally and then passed down to the Church. In fact, he did not hesitate to conclude that these methods represent "an apostolical rule for dispensing the word of life; and as such, the ancient Fathers received them." Armed with this conclusion, we can find ourselves looking at the teaching phase of Christ's work with his disciples in a whole new light.

There's no doubt that Newman's assessment, if proved true, would go a long way toward clarifying one of the most traditionally puzzling aspects of the Gospel accounts: our Lord's insistence on doing most of his public teaching by means of strange metaphors and obscure parables rather than simply doling out straightforward didactic answers about himself and his mission. If the Parable of the Unjust Judge (Luke 18:1–8) is meant to teach the lesson "You must be persistent in prayer and not give up," why not simply say "You must be persistent in prayer and not give up"? If the Parable of the Ten Virgins (Matt. 25:1–13) is meant to express the idea that, "Someday, long after my death, resurrection, and ascension back to heaven, I, Jesus, will return to judge humanity and those who have shown constancy and faith in the interval will have a leg up"—then why didn't he just say this in so many words? Did Jesus even *want* to be understood?

The answer to that question, surprisingly—and proved out by his own words—is *yes and no.* "Then the disciples came and said to him, 'Why do you speak to them in parables?' And he answered them, 'To you it has been given to know the secrets of the kingdom of heaven, but to them it has not been given. For to him who has will more be given, and he will have abundance; but from him who has not, even what he has will be taken away'" (Matt. 13:12). Jesus not only seems to be deliberately obscure in his teaching—he *tells us* that he is being deliberately obscure!

"'For those outside,'" he continues, "everything is in parables; so that they may indeed see but not perceive, and may indeed hear but not understand; lest they should turn again, and be forgiven'" (Mark 4:12). But wasn't that the whole purpose of his mission—that sinners should hear the gospel, receive it, and be converted? Maybe so, but Christ definitely begins his lessons to the disciples on an entirely different note: "Do not give what is holy to dogs; and do not throw your pearls before swine, or they will trample them under foot and turn and maul you" (Matt. 7:6).

The uncharacteristic harshness we may note in these sayings, toward people whose chief fault in our eyes seems to be mere ignorance, turned out to be the very thing that rang the bell for Newman. He perceived the unmistakable echoes of the *Disciplina* in phrases about a catechumen who "does not deserve" to hear and "strangers" whom Jesus has "not yet trusted." The earliest surviving reference to the *Disciplina*, in fact, evokes the "pearls before swine" principle in so many words. Tertullian, writing about A.D. 197, complains that the discipline of heretical groups was lax in this regard, causing holy things to be profaned: "Among them it is doubtful who is a catechumen and who a believer; all can come in alike; they hear side by side and pray together; even heathens, if any chance to come in. That which is holy they cast to the dogs, and their pearls . . . they fling to the swine." Many of the other Fathers used the same stern quotation to justify their practice.

When, however, Clement of Alexandria cited the same text not long after Tertullian, he included additional thoughts that help us discern the rationale behind the reticence. "We must hide that wisdom, spoken in mystery," he writes, "which the Son of God has taught us. Thus the Prophet Esaias has his tongue cleansed with fire, that he may be able to declare the vision;[39] and our ears must be sanctified as well as our tongues, if we aim at being recipients of the truth." This awareness, Clement continues, was actually "a hindrance to my [catechetical] writing; and still I have anxiety, since Scripture says, 'Cast not your pearls before swine;' for those pure and bright truths, which are so marvelous and full of God to goodly natures, do but provoke laughter, when spoken in the hearing of the many."

Far from hindering or dissuading them, Clement believed that he was *helping* his beginning students by withholding their exposure to more advanced lessons. St. Cyril adds more along the same lines: "What is the blaze of divine glory to the enlightened is the blinding of unbelievers.

39 A reference to Isaiah 6.

These are the secrets which the Church unfolds to him who passes on from the catechumens, and not to the heathen. For we do not unfold to a heathen the truths concerning Father, Son, and Holy Spirit; nay, not even in the case of catechumens, do we clearly explain the mysteries, but we frequently say many things indirectly, so that believers who have been taught may understand, and the others may not be injured."

So, in their evangelizing efforts, Newman concluded, "the Fathers would write, not with the openness of Christian familiarity, but with the tenderness or the reserve with which we are accustomed to address those who do not sympathize with us, or whom we fear to mislead or to prejudice against the truth, by precipitate disclosures of its details." Whence had they acquired this rule? "The example of the inspired writer of the epistle to the Hebrews was their authority for making a broad distinction between the doctrines suitable to the state of the weak and ignorant, and those which are the peculiar property of a baptized and regenerate Christian."

"In that epistle," Newman continues, "when speaking of the most sacred Christian verities, as hidden under the allegories of the Old Testament, the apostle seems suddenly to check himself, from worry that he was divulging mysteries beyond the understanding of his brethren . . . He speaks of the difference of doctrine suited respectively to neophytes and confirmed Christians, under the analogy of the difference of food proper for the old and young; a difference which lies, not in the arbitrary will of the dispenser, but in the necessity of the case, the more sublime truths of revelation affording no nourishment to the souls of the unbelieving or unstable." Here is the passage to which Newman refers: "But you need milk, not solid food; for everyone who lives on milk is unskilled in the word of righteousness, for he is a child. But solid food is for the mature, for those who have their faculties trained by practice to distinguish good from evil" (Heb. 5:7-14).

Newman found the same thought elsewhere in the Pauline writings: "The first epistle to the Corinthians contains the same distinction between the carnal or imperfect and the established Christian, which is laid down in that addressed to the Hebrews." He refers specifically to 1 Corinthians 2:1–14: "'Now we have received not the spirit of the world, but the Spirit which is from God, that we might understand the gifts bestowed on us by God. And we impart this in words not taught by human wisdom but taught by the Spirit, interpreting spiritual truths to those who possess the Spirit. The unspiritual man does not receive the gifts of the Spirit of God, for they are folly to him, and he is not able to understand them because they are spiritually discerned.'"

We see here that Paul considered the presence of the Holy Spirit in our lives to be absolutely necessary for understanding Christian doctrine in anything but a carnal or merely exterior way.

This idea that the apostles (not just the twelve but their later co-worker Paul as well) received a private, fuller initiation from Jesus which they later imparted to disciples of their own is strongly implied in Gospel passages such as Mark 4:3-4: "With many such parables he spoke the word to [the people], as they were able to hear it; he did not speak to them without a parable, but privately to his own disciples he explained everything."

The process is illustrated most clearly in Christ's Parable of the Weeds (Matt. 13). First, the public part of the story:

"The kingdom of heaven may be compared to a man who sowed good seed in his field; but while men were sleeping, his enemy came and sowed weeds among the wheat, and went away. So when the plants came up and bore grain, then the weeds appeared also. And the servants of the householder came and said to him, "Sir, did you not sow good seed in your field? How then has it weeds?" He said to them, "An enemy has done this." The servants said to him, "Then do you want us to go and gather them?" But he said, "No; lest in gathering the weeds you root up the wheat along with them. Let both grow together until the harvest; and at harvest time I will tell the reapers, Gather the weeds first and bind them in bundles to be burned, but gather the wheat into my barn" (Matt. 13:24-30).

Then later, while sequestered with the apostles in a private home, Jesus provides the "straight answer" that the crowd had been denied:

And his disciples came to him, saying, "'Explain to us the parable of the weeds of the field." He answered, "He who sows the good seed is the Son of Man; the field is the world, and the good seed means the sons of the kingdom; the weeds are the sons of the evil one, and the enemy who sowed them is the devil; the harvest is the close of the age, and the reapers are angels. Just as the weeds are gathered and burned with fire, so will it be at the close of the age. The Son of Man will send his angels, and they will gather out of his kingdom all causes of sin and all evildoers, and throw them into the furnace of fire; there men will weep and gnash their teeth. Then the righteous will shine like the sun in the kingdom of their Father. He who has ears, let him hear" (Matt. 13:36-43).

This last phrase—"he who has ears to hear"—was, of course, a favorite with our Lord during his earthly ministry; but notice that we have also seen it powerfully echoed in both apostolic and post-apostolic sources:

"With many such parables he spoke the word to them, *as they were able to hear it.*"

"Solid food is for those who have their *faculties trained by practice.*"

"*Our ears must be sanctified* if we aim at being recipients of the truth."

To illustrate, St. Paul's "gospel message" to the pagan governor Felix (Acts 23) commends efforts to keep "a clear conscience toward God and toward men"; and the only theological content in it is an affirmation of rewards and punishments after death—a tenet widely accepted even by pagans at the time. The deeper truths, in short, were God's reward for having learned the simpler; and theology, in the early Church, was kept "in house." "The early evangelists," according to Newman, considered their cautious methods to be "the most truly charitable consideration for those whom they addressed, who were likely to be perplexed, not converted, by the sudden exhibition of the whole evangelical scheme."

The Fathers translated these apostolic examples into a careful, gradual plan of Christian formation. This season of preparation (which the early Church called the *catechumenate*) was a sort of spiritual boot camp, a period of probation, of proving oneself serious . . . because being serious was the only thing that could render subsequent lessons profitable.

During the earliest stage of catechesis, according to Newman, "the chief subjects . . . were the doctrines of repentance and pardon, of the necessity of good works, of the nature and use of baptism, and the immortality of the soul—as the apostle had determined them." Catechists had to resist the urge to dispense with the lower steps of the ladder, to rush past them to theological mysteries. "Should a catechumen ask thee what the teachers have determined," counseled Cyril to his trainees, "tell nothing to one who is without. For we impart to thee a secret and a promise of the world to come. Keep safe the secret for him who gives the reward. Listen not to one who asks, 'What harm is there in my knowing also?' Even the sick ask for wine, which, unseasonably given, brings on delirium; and so there come two ills, the death of the patient and the disrepute of the physician."

The result of this reticence is striking indeed to modern eyes. "Even to the last," writes Newman, "they were granted nothing beyond a formal and general account of the articles of the Christian faith; the exact and fully developed doctrines of the Trinity and the Incarnation, and still more, the doctrine of the Atonement, as once made upon the cross, and commemorated and appropriated in the Eucharist, being the exclusive possession of the serious and practiced Christian." Hard as it is for us to imagine, the entire two-year (or more) period of the catechumenate passed without a single explicit statement about Original Sin, the divinity of Christ, the Person of the Holy Spirit, or salvation by grace.

But had the Savior really applied these methods to his own men? Weren't the fishermen of Galilee, weren't Nathaniel and Thomas, Jude and Simon, and the rest, beginners in all this as much as anyone else? How had they come so quickly to merit "straight answers" in private interviews? By what process had their "faculties been trained"? The answer may lie in a careful revisiting of the details of our story so far—as seen through the lens of the *Disciplina*.

If the masses hearing the message of Jesus were "cold," it was only because they had spurned the preparatory training of his predestined forerunner, John the Baptizer; he whose God-given task had been to "go before the Lord to prepare his ways, to give knowledge of salvation to his people in the forgiveness of their sins" (Luke 1:76-79). With John, they would have heard all the preliminaries needed to safely receive the elements of Christianity: the longstanding Essene dogmas about the coming day of the Lord, the resurrection of the body, the sacrifice of bread and wine, and the rest. Yes, the mere curiosity-seekers turned out in droves for the spectacle of Jesus' miracles, but these were, for the most part, the people who *had not* turned out for the baptism of John—who had exhibited only sincerity and truth. Pretty much everybody was interested in how the new messianic claimant would answer the many questions about his mission—but not many had a healthy, *holy* interest. For most, it was idle curiosity, an itch to keep current with "the latest thing," tainted with purely earthly concerns, tangled up in party politics. Jesus had come to graduate John's grade-schoolers to the new high school of his own tutelage; but most members of these mobs had never worked hard enough to pass kindergarten.

For this reason, all that "Jesus said to the crowds" he said "in parables; indeed he said nothing to them without a parable" (Matt. 13-34). An engaging story, the meaning of which might seem only just out of reach, would have the effect of stimulating further interest in those for whom hope was not yet lost. By withholding theology and offering narrative instead, our Lord could sneak "past watchful dragons," as C.S. Lewis described the method as he employed it while writing his Narnia fables: allowing the underlying theme of an interesting tale to seep under the reader's skin, so to speak, before the author mounts any attempt to penetrate his obstinate brain. Those of his hearers who, on the other hand, simply "spent their time in nothing else, but either to tell, or to hear some new thing" (Acts 17:21)—these would likely turn away from Christ's parables with frustration, having "seen without seeing, heard without having understood," annoyed, like Cyril's sick man begging for wine, that their impatient demands for a simple flow chart with clear bullet points had been perversely withheld.

Hardly any of our twelve, however, had *ever* heard Jesus "cold"—or if they had, they didn't remember. Even those who were not his kin, knowing him since childhood, probably received the Baptizer's own considered endorsement as they were being introduced to his messianic cousin. The idea, at any rate, that Jesus walked up to total (and totally uncatechized) strangers and said, "Follow me," is, in almost every case, an entirely false impression created by reading the passages out of their proper context.

Lack of historical context—specifically, lack of context for the status of the Bible at that time—also obscures the fact that the "apostolical rule for dispensing the word of life" was maintained *throughout* the lives of the apostles. Wouldn't the New Testament epistles have acted as a quick, easy cheat-sheet for getting around the Church's "discipline of secrecy"? After all, the deeper truths are written down there in black and white. This mistaken idea is created by nothing more than anachronism. Because the Bible is so public today—with a cheap Gideon's edition available in every roadside motel room—it gives the impression of having always been an open book to everyone. This, of course, is not so.

To begin with, none of the New Testament books were even composed until A.D. 50 or so, fifteen years or more after our Lord's Ascension; until that time the Gospel was preached and the world "turned upside down" (Acts 17:6) by *oral tradition* alone—the memories, that is, and the training, of the twelve apostles. "Accordingly," writes apologist Dave Armstrong, "when the phrases 'word of God' or 'word of the Lord' occur in Acts and the epistles, they almost always refer to oral preaching, not to the written word of the Bible, as many . . . casually assume."[xiii]

And even after the individual books and epistles did begin to appear (over a period of as much as fifty years), they were still kept, just like Clement's catechetical lessons, entirely "in house." In an age without printing, handwritten copies were sent out to the bishops presiding over the churches of the world, where the contents could be disseminated to their congregations at a pace determined by them. Literacy still being an art learned only by the highly educated, these elders and their trained lectors read the Gospels and the other books aloud to the faithful, sometimes translating them on the fly to parishioners who did not understand the Greek in which they were written. Even still, much of the contents of the sacred books was kept away from beginners for centuries. Only after making considerable progress were catechumens designated as *euchomenoi* (or "hearers")—allowed to stay, that is, for the reading of Scripture in church.

An awareness of these practices also goes a long way toward explaining another commonly heard misunderstanding about Jesus and his message. The superficial dissimilarities between the style and tone of the Gospels and that of the other New Testament books has led some to theorize that the apostles and other epistolary writers foisted, on their own authority, an alien complexity onto what was originally a much simpler body of teaching. The Beatitudes, the Golden Rule, "Love thy neighbor," and so forth, are held to be the authentic sayings of a wise, serene, and supremely simple prophet or sage who taught an easily understood message of universal brotherhood. All the tangled theologies and obscure dogmas, it is said, come in only with the later commentary, clearly the work of lesser hands. Our own Thomas Jefferson expressed the theory well when he shared, with distinguished and likeminded friends such as Joseph Priestly and John Adams, his plan to create a decidedly abridged edition of the New Testament for his own use:

> We must reduce our volume to the simple evangelists, select, even from them, the very words only of Jesus . . . [whose teachings] have been disfigured by the corruptions of schismatizing followers, who have found an interest in sophisticating and perverting the simple doctrines he

> taught, by engrafting on them the mysticisms of a Grecian sophist (Plato), frittering them into subtleties and obscuring them with jargon."[xiv]

In light of the *Disciplina*, however, it is easy to discern the real explanation for the disparity of tone that Jefferson noted: "To you it has been given to know the secrets of the kingdom of heaven, but to them it has not been given." There is no need to imagine two different gospels, one simple and the other complex, being dispensed by two different types of teacher, when the existence of two different types of *pupil*, at two different stages of formation, explains everything. *See Spot Run*, after all, is a very different book than *Moby Dick*—but both are examples, broadly speaking, of English literature. The synoptic Gospels seem to have been prepared for use by evangelists and the new, inexperienced laity who resulted from their work. As such, they include material suitable for those purposes and leave out material that was considered, as you'll recall Newman putting it, "the exclusive possession of the serious and practiced Christian . . . explained to the elders of the churches in the various New Testament epistles."

The disciples were being discipled for a reason. Unlike many religious founders, Jesus wrote down nothing at all. *His message was in the men.* He did not find it therein, he *poured* it . . . and as he did, he modeled his own divine teaching methodology for their eventual imitation. And when he was gone, the living safety deposit box he prepared could be opened—and *was* opened when the apostles opened their hearts to the churches of the world:

"God was in Christ reconciling the world to himself, not counting their trespasses against them, and entrusting to us the message of reconciliation. So we are ambassadors for Christ, God making his appeal through us" (2 Cor. 5:19-20).

5

LORD OF THE SABBATH

"Now while the Pharisees were gathered together, Jesus asked them a question, saying, 'What do you think of the Christ? Whose son is he?'"

—MATTHEW 22:41-42

Why do disputes with the Pharisees take up so much space in the Gospels?

Large portions of those sacred books can, at times, seem like little more than a series of unpleasant encounters with the existing religious authorities—not most people's idea of inspirational reading. To the casual student, Jesus almost seems to be deliberately antagonizing them, arranging times and circumstances for his miracles that were certain to provoke not just debate but opposition.

In Luke's Gospel, our Lord chooses the twelve apostles, then sets out immediately on a veritable crime wave of lawbreaking (or what certainly seemed to be lawbreaking in the eyes of the scribes and Pharisees). While healing a leper, "he touched him" (Luke 5:13), which an ordinary Hebrew holy man would not have done; touching lepers was against Moses' law.[40] At one of the synagogues, he encounters a man with a withered hand, "and the scribes and the Pharisees watched him, to see whether he would heal on the Sabbath" (Luke 6:17), an act that they judged to be "work" on a day when, according to the Third Commandment, no work must be done.

So why would Jesus set up such ugly clashes over Moses' law? And why do these questions loom so large in the Gospels? The answer is actually pretty simple: he did it because *all of the old rules were changing now*—and changing because of his arrival. "The law and the prophets were until John [the Baptist]," as Jesus informed the irate Pharisees; "since then the good news of the kingdom of God is preached, and every one enters it violently" (Luke 16:16). Many commentators have interpreted this notoriously difficult final phrase to mean "with upheavals," with "wrenching readjustments." Those who seek to enter Christ's new messianic kingdom must, in other words, not expect the change to come easily.

Jesus' relationship to Moses and his law was simply the pressing issue of the hour and the questions being asked by the Pharisees were the same ones to which all the rest of Israel—including the twelve apostles—were going to need answered sooner or later. By answering the Pharisees, then, Jesus answers his twelve witnesses as well . . . those who, we shall see, are being groomed as their replacements. Both groups, it's true, saw the same wonders, heard the same profound teaching, perceived the same gentleness and

40 Leviticus 13:45: "Now the leper on whom the sore is, his clothes shall be torn and his head bare; and he shall . . . cry, 'Unclean! Unclean!' He shall be unclean. All the days he has the sore he shall be unclean. He is unclean, and he shall dwell alone; his dwelling shall be outside the camp."

compassion in Jesus. Yet the twelve asked their questions with patience; the Pharisees, with hostility. What made the difference between those two responses? That's a subject too deep for quick, easy answers; but the beginnings of an explanation may be glimpsed, perhaps, by calling to mind one of Upton Sinclair's pithier quotes: "It is difficult to get a man to understand something when his job depends on not understanding it."

The twelve, we mustn't forget, had been zealous Law-keepers themselves, just as much as the Pharisees. Not only our rabbinical student Nathanael but most of the other apostles, too, give recognizable signs of being well-versed in the Law and zealous about its keeping. Andrew's brother Simon retained so much of this zeal that he keeps strictly kosher for a long while even after Christ's return to heaven; and even during a heavenly vision on the topic, in which he is encouraged to "loosen up" and enjoy Gentile foods, he is willing to aver, "By no means, Lord; for I have never eaten anything that is profane or unclean" (Acts 10:4).

The New Six (whom we mentioned a few pages back to fill out Jesus' final roster) all show signs of ardent Judaism as well. James, the son of Alphaeus (often called "the lesser James" to distinguish him from the better-known son of Zebedee) and Judas (commonly referred to these days as St. Jude, from the Latin form of the name, to keep him separate from the traitor) may both have been part of that "royal family" of which we spoke; and "we may venture to assert that their training . . . had been that which prevailed in all pious Jewish homes and that it was therefore based on the knowledge of the holy Scripture and the rigorous observance of the Law."[xv] Thomas and Simon Zealotes seem to have been Galilean fishermen along with the first group recruited by Jesus—and therefore likely to have been, like them, steeped in the same "Essenism by way of John the Baptist" theology. Matthew the tax collector (known as "Levi" in Mark and Luke) appears to have been enlisted to the apostolic college by our Lord directly, without first having been a mere disciple.

Not only had most of the apostles kept the law of Moses before they met Christ, but their keeping of it made them worthy of the fuller revelations they received when he came. We see this principle at work in the lives of Zechariah and Elizabeth, parents of the Baptizer, who "were righteous before God, living blamelessly according to all the commandments and regulations of the Lord" (Luke 1:6). And however often it is disparaged in sloppy sermons about "legalism," during the Old Covenant era the careful keeping of Moses' multitudinous regulations really was the key to blessing; of this, Scripture leaves no doubt. "This book of the law," commanded Joshua, "shall not depart out of your mouth; you shall meditate on it day and night, so that you may be careful to act in accordance with all that is written in it. For then you shall make your way prosperous, and then you shall be successful" (Josh. 1:8-9).

Moses himself, even after giving the much fuller and more onerous "second law" contained in the book of Deuteronomy, says, "This entire commandment that I command you today, you must diligently observe, so that you may live and increase, and go in and occupy the land that the Lord promised on oath to your ancestors . . . You must neither add anything to what I command you nor take away anything from it, but keep the commandments of the LORD your God with which I am charging you" (Deut. 8:1, 4:2).

Neglect of the Law, on the other hand, had always been recognized as the sure pathway to chastisement and disaster.

Deuteronomy 28, for instance, follows up its wonderful promises of blessing with a litany of truly horrific curses:

> But if you will not obey the Lord your God by diligently observing all his commandments and decrees, which I am commanding you today, then all these curses shall come upon you and overtake you . . . The Lord will send upon you disaster, panic, and frustration in everything you attempt to do, until you are destroyed and perish quickly, on account of the evil of your deeds, because you have forsaken me . . . The Lord will make the pestilence cling to you until it has consumed you off the land that you are entering to possess. The Lord will afflict you with consumption, fever, inflammation, with fiery heat and drought, and with blight and mildew; they shall pursue you until you perish. The sky over your head shall be bronze, and the earth under you iron. The Lord will change the rain of your land into powder, and only dust shall come down upon you from the sky until you are destroyed . . . All these curses shall come upon you, pursuing and overtaking you until you are destroyed, because you did not obey the Lord your God, by observing the commandments and the decrees that he commanded you. They shall be among you and your descendants as a sign and a portent forever (Deut. 28:15-24, 45-46).

Indeed, no one who has read the whole of Deuteronomy 28 can ever again lightly charge the scribes and the Pharisees with mere scrupulosity or with being morbidly "hung up" on petty "religious rules." Yes, the religion of Moses contained a great deal more than *just* religious rules; but make no mistake—the rules were real and God definitely did mean them to be obeyed.

This is why even the apostles were confused by events such as the one that occurred at the pool of Bethesda in Jerusalem. There, Jesus healed a lame man (on the Sabbath, of course) by telling him, "Stand up, take your mat and walk." There was, perhaps, some legitimate debate over whether a miracle of healing constitutes a "work" or not; one often hears this argued, as the apostles may have heard it in their day. But rolling up a mat and carrying it away? Nathanael, at least, could have cited chapter and verse against this, if not most of his companions as well.[41] Yahweh himself ordered a man stoned to death for carrying a bundle of wood on the Sabbath! (Num. 15:32-36). Jeremiah renewed the same stricture in his day while reminding his own careless generation about Moses' law: "Thus says the Lord: For the sake of your lives, take care that you do not bear a burden on the Sabbath day or bring it in by the gates of Jerusalem. And do not carry a burden out of your houses on the Sabbath or do any work, but keep the Sabbath day holy, as I commanded your ancestors" (Jer. 17:21).

The Nazarene's command then, seemed not only lawless but deliberately provocative. His disciples had seen too many signs to give up on him quickly . . . but there's little use pretending they wouldn't have been bewildered by this kind of stuff, perhaps even scandalized. Certainly, a great many others were.

Jesus' own response to the Pharisees, when called out

41 "Chapter and verse" is used as a figure of speech here; these conveniences weren't actually added to our Bibles until many centuries later.

about the healing at the pool, was unexpected, puzzling . . . but also suggested great depths of meaning. "Jesus answered them, 'My Father is still working, and I also am working'" (John 5:17). God then, keeps working on the Sabbath—for how, otherwise, could the stars and planets keep their courses, or we ourselves remain in existence? But wait . . . was this really the carpenter of Nazareth claiming God's own privileges? "For this reason," John continues, "the Jews were seeking all the more to kill him, because he was not only breaking the Sabbath, but was also calling God his own Father, thereby making himself equal to God" (v. 18)—an act that (unless it were true, of course—an absurdity to be discounted) would constitute the worst sin of all. For many readers through the centuries, seeking to kill Jesus for this may have seemed a bizarre overreaction—even a jealous vendetta; but those who remember that hapless fellow gathering wood in Numbers 15 have seen the other side of the story.

On this point at least, the Gospel's "bad guys" have gotten a bit of a bum rap. Jesus faults them for *hypocrisy,* yes—for laying grievous burdens on men's shoulders while "you yourselves touch not the burdens with one of your fingers" (Luke 11:46, KJV)—but he never blames them for enjoining strict law-keeping *per se.* In fact, he endorses it outright at one point, even in a matter that seems trifling indeed to the non-Jewish reader: "Woe to you, scribes and Pharisees, hypocrites! For you tithe mint, dill, and cummin, and have neglected the weightier matters of the law: justice and mercy and faith. It is these you ought to have practiced without neglecting the others" (Matt. 23:23). The hesitancy then, of the Israelites to countenance from a messianic claimant behavior that had always been seen as sin in the past, is not difficult to understand. The prophets had done too good a job up fixing the blame for all their current misfortunes on past desertion of God's law. Not even the apostles could yet grasp who exactly they were dealing with in Jesus of Nazareth . . . and it just so happened that his case for "breaking" the law turns on just that crucial point.

The apostles themselves finally became implicated in all the lawbreaking . . . and it's a good thing for us that they did, because the event in question contains the key to the whole problem. The story is told in all three synoptic Gospels; here is Mark's account:

> One Sabbath he was going through the grainfields; and as they made their way his disciples began to pluck heads of grain. And the Pharisees said to him, "Look, why are they doing what is not lawful on the Sabbath?" And he said to them, "Have you never read what David did, when he was in need and was hungry, he and those who were with him: how he entered the house of God, when Abiathar was high priest, and ate the bread of the Presence, which it is not lawful for any but the priests to eat, and also gave it to those who were with him?" And he said to them, "The Sabbath was made for man, not man for the Sabbath; so the Son of Man is lord even of the Sabbath" (Mark 2:23-28).

Did thunder rumble in the distance as Jesus pronounced this last phrase? It would certainly have been appropriate if it did, since to be "lord" over something is, in this sense, to be its ruler, its absolute master . . . and every Hebrew in Palestine knew very well that it was God himself who had instituted the Sabbath, on the seventh day of creation. Yes, Jesus presents a less astounding argument as well (though still startling enough to his contemporaries): *King David did this without your criticizing him, therefore I, Jesus, David's successor can do it, too.* Technically speaking, Hebrew priests profaned the Sabbath every week by working to replace the showbread in the tabernacle; and after the new loaves were set out, the priests ate the old ones (Exod. 25:30, Lev. 24:5-9). David—who cannot have been a priest in the ordinary sense; a priest, that is, after the order of Aaron (he belonged to the wrong family, that of Judah)—laid claim to this priestly privilege by eating the showbread himself and even offering it to his men.[42] Now, Jesus (also a Judahite, not a Levite) asserts for himself membership in the same "new extraordinary priesthood" to which his forefather David had prophetically laid claim. But "lord of the Sabbath" was something else again.

That title implied another argument altogether, an argument too flabbergasting for most Jews to entertain long enough to even put into words. "I, Jesus," said the Nazarene in essence, "am lord of the Sabbath; and as such, I am sovereign over it. It's mine; and I will do with it as I please, with or without your leave. If I keep its restrictions, I keep them because *I choose to do so*; not because they will make me good or because not keeping them would make me a sinner, but simply because it is seemly for me to do so for the time being, just as it was becoming of me to accept the baptism of John. But make no mistake: Moses' law does not apply to me now and never did apply. Moses was not lord of the Sabbath—he would have rent his garments, in fact, had anyone dared to call him that—but *I am*. I can dispense my servants from some of it, or all of it. I can even abrogate it altogether if I so choose, so that it will apply in its original form to *no*

42 Notice that Jesus is not only associating himself with David but associated his men with David's; those same men for whom we saw Abigail arranging provisions back in chapter 2.

one any longer—not even to you Jews. *If I so choose.* This is what I, Jesus, mean by "lord of the Sabbath."[43]

Certainly a neat, tidy answer—but what an answer!

This is what was meant by asserting that the solution to the problem of our Lord's so-called lawbreaking turns on nothing less than a correct appraisal of his own identity. What Jesus was doing and saying couldn't ultimately be separated from the question of *who Jesus is*—and that was the whole difficulty in a nutshell. The *Catechism of the Catholic Church* (CCC), explains the lawbreaking problem in this way: "In presenting with divine authority the definitive interpretation of the Law, Jesus found himself confronted by certain teachers of the Law who did not accept his interpretation . . . guaranteed though it was by the divine signs that accompanied it" (582). *Were* the signs, in fact, divine? And in what sense? On these kinds of questions hung all his right to appropriate that astounding title—lord of the Sabbath—and without that right his appropriation is usurpation. And yes, blasphemy. Confronting the absurdity they thought could be "discounted" was (and still is) absolutely inescapable.

The apostles were the first to confront this Sphinx's Riddle For them, there was no getting away from it, since the devils had been screeching it in their ears for weeks! "And

---

43 It should be noted that the original Sabbath of Genesis is not simply identical with the Mosaic Law-Sabbath laid out in the book of Deuteronomy, which added dozens of difficult regulations to the bare idea of a sacred day of rest. This recognition captures the essence of what St. Paul meant by writing, in Galatians 3:19, about a Law that "was added because of transgressions." The original primordial Law cannot pass away but only the later, more vexing codes of Deuteronomy which were laid on "because of the hardness of your hearts" (Matt. 19:8). That "Second Legislation," as the Fathers called it, was only "till the offspring should come"—indicating that Moses' Law had a temporary lifespan built into it from the beginning with an expiration date tied to the advent of Messiah. For those interested in exploring this vital (but admittedly difficult) subject more closely, the author recommends his earlier book *Scripture Wars: How Justin Martyr Rescued the Old Testament for Christians.*

demons," Luke records, "came out of many, crying, 'You are the Son of God!' But he [Jesus] rebuked them, and would not allow them to speak, because they knew that he was the Christ" (Luke 4:41). Again we wonder, as we wondered in the previous chapter, whether that wasn't the whole point—that sinners should accept Jesus as Messiah and be converted?

Yet the apostles knew already that many of his miracles had been accompanied by this same demand for secrecy. When he raised the daughter of Jairus from the dead, "her parents were amazed; but he charged them to tell no one what had happened" (Luke 8:56). And then, speaking to witnesses at Decapolis, where he opened the ears of a deaf man, "he charged them to tell no one; but the more he charged them, the more zealously they proclaimed it" (Mark 7:36). It appears that Jesus really did seek to control the time and the pace at which the profounder facts about himself were revealed (see also Luke 8:56).

Yet what did "Son of God" really mean in this context? As we've seen, Nathanael of Cana was able to cry out, at the very *beginning* of his journey without any training from Jesus at all, "Rabbi, you are the Son of God! You are the king of Israel!" And in that private setting, Jesus accepted the affirmation and made no attempt to shush the confessor. What, at that early stage, had Nathanael meant by the term?

Son of God, according to the old *Catholic Encyclopedia*, was a title "applied in the Old Testament to persons having any special relationship with God." In the book of Job, for instance, the angels who present themselves before the Lord are called "sons of God" (1:6). "Angels, just and pious men, the descendants of Seth," the *Encyclopedia* continues, "were called 'sons of God' (Job 1:6; 2:1; Psalm 89:7; Wis. 2:13; etc.). In a similar manner it was given to Israelites (Deut. 14:50); and of Israel, as a nation, we read: 'And thou shalt say to him: Thus saith the Lord: Israel is my son, my firstborn.

I have said to thee: Let my son go, that he may serve me' (Exod. 4:22). The leaders of the people, kings, princes, judges, as holding authority from God, were called sons of God."[xvi]

All this being the case, is it possible that Nathanael meant nothing more than "I accept you, Jesus, as our long-awaited messianic king"? Possible, yes—but to insist on that "nothing more" ignores the display of supernatural knowledge that occasioned his outcry and also the more advanced state of development that the term had reached by the eve of Christ's advent. "The theocratic king as lieutenant of God," often a type of the messiah to come, was also called Son of God in the Old Testament.[xvii] We've already imagined Nathanael interacting with perhaps the plainest example of this, Psalm 2:6-7—"I have set my king [David] on Zion, my holy hill . . . You are my son; today I have begotten you"—an excellent illustration of how the prophecies about "messiah as God's own Son" acquired a more literal meaning as time went on.

We need not assume then, that Nathanael was ready at that point to make anything like an exact affirmation of the divinity of Christ that would have passed the test of later Athanasian orthodoxy;[44] but he almost certainly did use "Son of God" to avow a newfound belief, at least, that the Nazarene must represent some kind of unique personification of God's saving purpose.

It was a start, anyhow.

The trouble with "Son of God"—the reason Jesus avoids using the term himself, and the reason he responds so

44 The Athanasian Creed is a venerable expression of the Church's mature conclusions about the Trinity and the Incarnation. Probably not the work of the great Athanasius himself, it likely dates from the fifth century.

evasively when outsiders try to pin him down on it (Cf. Matt. 26:61-64; Luke 22:69-71; John 10:31-39)—must surely lie in the fact that the title itself can present such a roadblock to understanding. It's a simple fact that of the hundred or more different ways that "Son of God" has been interpreted in the centuries since—even by very sincere Christians—ninety-nine of them are wrong! Are we to take the designation at face value—that Jesus is the offspring of a physical union between his young Jewish mother Mary and the divine Father of the universe? That's certainly how potential pagan converts would have interpreted it, accustomed as they were to the tales of Leda and the Swan, of demigods such as Perseus or Heracles, the illegitimate sons of Zeus.

Or was Jesus an ordinary (if uniquely virtuous) human being who *became God* by adoption—possibly at his baptism? If not, then perhaps the "Son of God" is a kind of Xerox copy of the original, uncreated God, custom-made by him to save the world. Or maybe "Son of God" is just a persona that our heavenly Father adopts in certain circumstances, a convenient interface for communicating with fallen humanity? Then again, perhaps Jesus is a human being in whom the pre-existing divine spirit called "God the Son" has taken the place normally occupied by a human soul—God wearing an Earth-suit, so to speak?

Odd as these expedients sound today, each and every one of them has been employed by various movements in Church history in efforts to avoid what seemed to them to be the only other, even more shocking "face value" conclusion: that when the Son of God arrived at Bethlehem, it meant that an actual *second God* was born into the universe.

The bottom line is that the mystery of the divine Sonship was and is an exceptionally difficult reality to grasp without making mistakes, even for those fully on board with "Jesus as Messiah." The Church Catholic wrestled with all of these faulty formulas in its own struggle to keep its head on the subject, and the process took literal centuries. Small wonder that our Lord hesitated to see it thrown indiscriminately to the mob at the very start of the process!

If this is true, however, why did the Nazarene keep pushing the issue to the fore? If "Jesus is the divinely appointed instrument of our deliverance" was a valid starting point for Nathanael—a legitimate, if limited, interpretation of Jesus' identity and role—why not allow the nation to rally around him on that basis? Why not leave it at that—and save the more advanced lessons ("lord of the Sabbath," for instance) until after he had been crowned king?

At times, the apostles almost seem to be encouraging him to do just that—in difficult moments changing the subject to questions, for instance, about when exactly he was going to move on Jerusalem, or introducing sudden nonsensical disputes about which cabinet officer would outrank what general among them in the coming kingdom. Our Lord, however, *was not* content to leave it there. The principles of the *Disciplina* necessitated a cautious pace, yes; a teaching style aimed at raising the right questions at the right time rather than randomly casting pearls before swine. Yet the only way, really, to justify the outrageous things he was doing and saying about himself—including the authority he claimed to overrule Moses and institute a whole new covenant of salvation to replace the one given at Sinai—was to offer an outrageous defense. He must drive his hearers to confess, out of their own hearts, the sovereignty he was claiming for himself: not just God's messenger . . . but *God delivering a message.*

So Jesus walked a tightrope. He kept pushing the question forward, explosive as it was; kept arranging these ugly encounters and doing things that outraged the nation's existing religious sensibilities . . . because the only way out was *through.*

We might say that he *modeled* the answer to begin with, rather than expressing it verbally. For example, the public called him a prophet—but to a Scripture scholar like Nathanael, from his up-close-and-personal point of view within the apostolic band, it would have become slowly obvious that Jesus didn't behave like one of the prophets *at all.* When he said, "I am gentle and lowly in heart," for example, everyone believed him at once; he really was the tenderest, humblest man on earth. But after watching him closely for a while, his followers begin to notice how intensely "Jesus-centric" Jesus' teaching really was! "Come to me, all who labor and are heavy laden . . . I am the light of the world . . . He who finds his life will lose it, but he who loses his life for my sake will find it" (Matt. 11:28, John 8:12; Matt. 10:39). The other prophets and wise men had always been careful to direct people *away* from themselves and toward Yahweh. But Jesus, as Nathanael himself had experienced, not only accepted but actually encouraged devotion and loyalty to *his own person*, veneration bordering on actual worship: "He who does not take up his cross and follow me is not worthy of me . . . Every one who has left houses or brothers or sisters or father or mother or children or lands, for my name's sake, will receive a hundredfold, and inherit eternal life . . . He who is not with me is against me, and he who does not gather with me scatters" (Matt. 10:38, 19:29; Luke 11:23).

Even more alarming than his constant focus on himself, perhaps, was the fact that the Nazarene never seemed to own up to any weaknesses or confess any faults; just the opposite, in fact. "Which of you convicts me of sin?" he asked, when some of the Jews were inclined to question his word (John 8:46). "He that sent me is with me: the Father hath not left me alone; for I do always those things that please him" (John 8:29, KJV). Robert Hugh Benson expressed the paradox this way:

> If this Man were man only, however perfect and sublime, how is it that his sanctity appears to run by other lines than those of other saints? Other perfect men as they approached perfection were most conscious of imperfection; other saints as they were nearer God lamented their distance from him; other teachers of the spiritual life pointed always away from themselves and their shortcomings to that Eternal Law to which they too aspired. Yet with this Man all seems reversed. He, as he stood before the world, called on men to imitate him; not, as other leaders have done, to avoid his sins: this Man, so far from pointing forward and up, pointed to himself as the Way to the Father; so far from adoring a Truth to which he strove, named himself its very incarnation; so far from describing a life to which he too one day hoped to rise, bade his hearers look on himself Who was their life; so far from deploring to his friends the sins under which he labored, challenged his enemies to find within him any sin at all.[xviii]

His ongoing barrage of miracles, too, contrasted with Old Testament analogues—and not just in number. "Moses speaks hastily and acts unbelievingly (Num. 20:11)," writes Evangelical scholar Herbert Lockyer. "Elijah and Elisha had to pray long and put forth much effort in their miracle ministry (1 Kings 18:42-44; 2 Kings 4:31-35). Where the miracles are similar in kind, like the feeding of the hungry,

Christ's are larger, freer, and more glorious."[xix] This contrast, to open-minded observers, would have suggested that the "middle man" really had been eliminated somehow, and that Jesus' own words best explained the difference: "All things have been handed over to me by my Father . . . All authority in heaven and on earth has been given to me" (Matt. 11:27, 28:18). "Always be yourself" is a common piece of advice; to make a compelling *non-verbal* case for his own divine nature, Jesus had only to be himself in front of the watching world.

Gradually, however, the words do come . . . but even then, our Lord's first inclination is to employ them as a way to arouse a hunger for the truth rather than to provide spoon-fed answers. "When the Son of Man comes in his glory, and all the angels with him," he told those assembled at the Mount of Olives, "then he will sit on the throne of his glory. All the nations will be gathered before him, and he will separate people one from another as a shepherd separates the sheep from the goats" (Matt. 25:31-32)—leaving his disciples, of course, to wonder what kind of man is holy enough to sit in judgment over the rest of mankind.

"The Son of Man will come with his angels in the glory of his Father," he told his disciples at Caesarea Philippi, "and then he will repay every man for what he has done" (Matt. 16:27). How exactly a faithful Jew was meant to square this statement with one of God's most famous prerogatives from the book of Deuteronomy—*Vengeance is mine, I will repay*—the Nazarene left for his hearers to puzzle out.

"I tell you, every one who acknowledges me before men, the Son of Man also will acknowledge before the angels of God; but he who denies me before men will be denied before the angels of God" (Luke 12:8). So a man's eternal soul could depend upon his fidelity—not to Moses' covenant or even to the God of Sinai himself—but to the name of Jesus from Galilee!

Striking as these statements are, they do still fall a bit short of "I am the co-eternal Second Person of the Holy Trinity come down from heaven." John's Gospel, here unquoted as yet, comes much closer in this regard—so much closer that it has presented a mystery to scholars through the years. The affirmations we find in those pages are plainer and far more abundant than those in the other three Gospels, with many more sayings of the type that, during our discussion of the *Disciplina,* we called straightforward, didactic, or theological:

"You are from below, I am from above; you are of this world, I am not of this world" (8:23).

"Father, the hour has come; glorify thy Son that the Son may glorify thee . . . glorify thou me in thy own presence with the glory which I had with thee before the world was made" (17:1, 5).

"If you know me, you will know my Father also. From now on you do know him and have seen him" (14:7).

And certainly the author of the Gospel, in his remarkable preface, appears to have had no worries at all about blinding his readers with St. Cyril's "blaze of divine glory":

> In the beginning was the Word, and the Word was with God, and the Word was God. He was in the beginning with God. All things came into being through him, and without him not one thing came into being . . . He was in the world, and the world came into being through him; yet the world did not know him . . . And the Word became flesh and lived among us, and we have seen his glory, the glory as of a father's only son, full of grace and truth.

How do we account for this very conspicuous difference? Because the Gospel of John was written some years after the other three (a fact conceded by the Church since the days of Origen), some scholars have gathered an impression that, over time, Jesus' followers got carried away with their praises. In fact, during the glory days of "higher criticism," a majority of scholars began to insist that the fourth Gospel must be a very late production indeed, dating from the mid-second century at the earliest, more likely the middle third![45] As the thinking went, John's more developed Christology supposedly proves that the author (certainly not St. John!) was interpolating the Church's later reflections on the life and teachings of the Nazarene rather than merely sharing an account of things he actually said and did.

The missing fact in all this? Neither Matthew's Gospel, nor Luke's, nor even that of St. Mark, is the earliest book of the New Testament! Yes, the four Gospels are given pride of place in our Bibles, but the New Testament is not arranged chronologically, on the basis of which book appeared first. The reality is that at least a handful of the New Testament epistles came before the Gospels. Many scholars think that Paul's first letter to the Thessalonians is the earliest Christian book, written about A.D. 50; others declare for the letter of James. The rest appeared one at a time in some order no longer known to us—but all during the same two decades, roughly A.D. 50 to 70, with the entire collection complete well before the author of the fourth Gospel ever put pen to parchment (before the end of the first century).

And these epistles mince no words about Jesus' divinity at all.

---

45 This notion has now been completely rejected. Dozens of new manuscript discoveries made in recent decades have strongly reaffirmed the traditional first-century dating of John's Gospel. In fact, the oldest surviving fragment of *any* New Testament book—Rylands Papyrus P52—is a section of John's Gospel dating from between 90-125; pretty much contemporary, that is, with the original.

"Long ago," writes the author of the letter to the Hebrews, "God spoke to our ancestors in many and various ways by the prophets, but in these last days he has spoken to us by a Son, whom he appointed heir of all things, through whom he also created the worlds. He is the reflection of God's glory and the exact imprint of God's very being, and he sustains all things by his powerful word" (1:1-3a). "His divine power," adds Simon Peter in one of his epistles, "has given us everything needed for life and godliness" (2 Pet. 1:3). "For in Christ," according to Paul, "all the fullness of the Deity lives in bodily form, and you have been given fullness in Christ, who is the head over every power and authority" (Col. 2:9). Jesus, "though he was in the form of God, did not regard equality with God as something to be grasped. Rather, he emptied himself, taking the form of a slave, coming in human likeness; and found in human appearance, he humbled himself, becoming obedient to death, even a death on the cross" (Phil. 2:6-9). These words are taken from *the oldest Christian documents in existence*—and those books affirm a strong belief in the divine Sonship of Jesus Christ.

So why *does* the Gospel of John sound so much franker and more upfront when it comes to this most crucial topic? What else can the answer be, in light of the ancient "rule of reticence" we've discovered, but that John wrote with *a different readership* in mind? No need to imagine two different Christs—one simple, comprehensible, and merely human, and a later Christ distorted and falsified by the jargon of schismatizing followers—when the idea of an "in-house" Gospel, mature and unexpurgated, carefully dispensed *to the churches only* by the apostles and their successors, explains everything. Here, the teaching included in the three synoptics and the more advanced sayings recorded in the fourth Gospel were both imparted to the apostles by the Lord *during the same earthly ministry*; the only difference is that those included in the book of John took a little longer to "reach print," so to speak.[46] This simplest explanation strongly underscores the conception of the twelve as Christ's own living safety deposit box . . . who only put his message into writing as circumstances dictated over the rest of the century.

For the Twelve, the learning process must have been quite the roller-coaster ride. Probably our Lord's most extreme claims sunk into the apostolic heads only very gradually . . . and their ability to untangle all the seeming contradictions must have waxed and waned. Just when his words made him seem most unearthly, perhaps, our Lord reshuffled the deck by doing some little thing that re-emphasized his obvious human ordinariness. He wept at the grave of a friend. He grew hungry and thirsty along the wayside, just as they did. His other bodily functions were normal, too, as those who spent practically every waking hour with him could hardly fail to have noticed! The Samaritan woman at Jacob's well recognized his Jewish ethnicity right away.

The process may have reached something of a climax at the end of one particular long day's preaching near the seashore: "On that day, when evening had come, he said to them, 'Let us go across to the other side.' And leaving the crowd, they took him with them, just as he was, in the boat." The blow that struck must have been sudden and unpredictable, since most of the twelve were experienced

46 The three synoptic Gospels were carefully tailored to suit their target readerships: Matthew's Gospel to be used by orthodox, ethnic Jews; Mark's for the Hellenized Jews of the Dispersion; and Luke's for quasi-Jewish God-fearers and pagan inquirers. John's Gospel has long been recognized as the outlier, written in a much more explicitly "theological" style and deliberately omitting most of the material covered elsewhere. These facts strongly suggest that the Gospel of John was prepared for use only by mature, catechized Christians—representing a complete "uncut" version of the story, so to speak, adding back in the "deleted scenes."

seamen. "And a great storm of wind arose, and the waves beat into the boat, so that the boat was already filling. But he was in the stern, asleep on the cushion; and they woke him and said to him, 'Teacher, do you not care if we perish?' And he awoke and rebuked the wind, and said to the sea, 'Peace! Be still!' And the wind ceased, and there was a great calm" (Mark 4:35-39).

No legion of angels called down for assistance. Not even a prayer to his Father for deliverance. He just did it himself. "He said to the sea . . ."

How did the apostles react?

"He said to them, 'Why are you afraid? Have you still no faith?' And they were filled with great awe and said to one another, 'Who then is this, that even the wind and the sea obey him?'" (Mark 4:40-41).

6
EXODUS

"No one has ascended into heaven but he who descended from heaven, the Son of Man. And as Moses lifted up the serpent in the wilderness, so must the Son of Man be lifted up, that whoever believes in him may have eternal life."

—John 3:13-15

Not long after the calming of the storm, our Lord was ready to broach the question with his chosen twelve directly: "Now when Jesus came into the district of Caesarea Philippi, he asked his disciples, 'Who do men say that the Son of Man is?' And they said, 'Some say John the Baptist, others say Elijah, and others Jeremiah or one of the prophets'" (Matt. 16:13-14). All of these popular beliefs, based on contemporary legends regarding an "end-times" reappearance of some eminent saint of the past, were totally off-base, of course. But, as St. John Chrysostom points out in his commentary on the passage, they were "at least relatively more free from malice than the opinions of the religious leaders, which were teeming with bad motives."[xx] Jesus clearly expects more, however, from his handpicked pupils. So, "He said to them, 'But who do you say that I am?'" (Matt. 16:15).

Notice that this is actually the apostles' own question—from when they had cried out in the boat, "Who then is this, that even wind and sea obey him?"—turned back on them. And yet they hesitate. The meteorological miracle that occasioned that original outburst seems so stupendous, so clearly beyond the scope of mortal man, that modern readers have often judged the twelve a little slow on the uptake here. Yet Moses once rearranged a sea without being God incarnate; and even his understudy Joshua duplicated the feat (on a smaller scale) when he parted the river Jordan so that the Ark of the Covenant might pass. Power over the forces of nature, then, even on an enormous scale, had *of itself* been no sign of divine Sonship so far. Thus, as Chrysostom continues, "Jesus probes for some other judgment from them . . . some higher mental picture."[xxi]

Finally, "Simon Peter replied, 'You are the Christ, the Son of the living God'" (Matt. 16:16–17) . . . and in doing so finally reaches, it would seem, the same point Nathanael had achieved by the end of chapter one! Yet we can tell from our Savior's response that practically the same words have somehow taken on a new significance. "And Jesus answered him, 'Blessed are you, Simon Bar-Jona! For flesh and blood has not revealed this to you, but my Father who is in heaven.'" The bare affirmation of messiahship that "Son of God" may once have carried has been overshadowed, at last, by a connotation large enough to suit the occasion.

Notice that Andrew's younger brother has not learned the great secret by diligent study, nor by natural intelligence; no bragging rights are in play, since our Lord explicitly attributes his disciple's truer answer to a supernatural outpouring of divine revelation. Even so, Simon's response does appear to merit a reward in our Lord's eyes; and it has revealed to him, it seems, an aptitude within the Big Fisherman for greater responsibilities in the future: "And I tell you, you are Peter,[47] and on this rock I will build my church, and the powers of death shall not prevail against it. I will give you the keys of the kingdom of heaven, and whatever you bind on earth shall be bound in heaven, and whatever you loose on earth shall be loosed in heaven."[48] Significantly, Jesus finishes the interview by repeating his now-familiar demand for secrecy: "Then he strictly charged the disciples to tell no one that he was the Christ" (Matt. 16:20).

Eight days later, Jesus took Peter, John, and James up on the mountain to pray" (Luke 9:28)—intentionally excluding nine of the twelve from witnessing the astonishing transfiguration that Jesus knew was about to take place there. This fact would seem to lend additional credence to the idea that our Savior continued to observe something like the *Disciplina Arcana* even this late into his lessons, disclosing his most prodigious revelations only to his most advanced pupils.[49] John was taken to the mountaintop, the natural-born mystic, traditional author of the profoundest

47 John's Gospel alone includes the Latinized spelling of *Cephas* (from Greek *Kephas*) in 1:42. Our English name Peter is derived from the Greek *Petros*, "a rock." Quibbles about whether the rock is a big one or a small one (often heard in anti-Catholic polemics) are beside the point when one considers that *Petros* itself was a substitution employed by the Evangelist (writing Greek) to stand-in for the actual name in spoken Aramaic: *Kepha*, which is simply "rock" freed from any ambiguities. John's Gospel emphasizes *Kephas* (in its Latinized form *Cephas*) when introducing this apostle (1:42); and St. Paul uses it almost exclusively.

48 Many good books have been written explaining the basis for Catholic distinctives about Peter and his successors. The author might specially recommend *Pope Peter* from Catholic Answers Press and *Upon This Rock: St. Peter and the Primacy of Rome in Scripture and the Early Church* from Ignatius Press. The subject is, at any rate, no part of our purpose in these pages.

49 According to Origen, "The text suggests that it would be possible for Jesus to be transfigured before some of his disciples, and not before others" (ACCS, NT Vol. II, pg. 110).

Gospel; the greater James was taken, probably a cousin and lifelong friend to our Lord; and Peter, keeper of the keys. "And as he was praying, the appearance of his countenance was altered, and his raiment became dazzling white"—as white as light, according to St. Matthew's version, and his face shone like the sun.

This change, the apostles will later realize, was not Jesus advancing to some new state of perfection or donning some new garment . . . but *dropping an old one*: "Rather," as we have already read, "he [had previously] emptied himself, taking the form of a slave, coming in human likeness . . . found in human appearance, he [had] humbled himself" It was a look that John would recognize when he saw it a second time many years later; a vision he records in the book of Revelation: "In his right hand he held seven stars . . . and his face was like the sun shining in full strength" (1:16).

"And behold, two men talked with [Jesus], Moses, and Elijah, who appeared in glory and spoke of his departure, which he was to accomplish at Jerusalem" (Luke 9:31). These two men, whose lives on earth had been separated by as much as 700 years, are here to stand in symbolically for the Law and the Prophets: the Old Covenant giving its stamp of approval to the New. If John felt a sense of déjà vu when he saw the glorified Christ again during the events of the Apocalypse, Moses must have undergone a similar experience here at the Transfiguration. Moses, recall, had once climbed to an awesome mountaintop, taken three trusted companions with him, and—as we shall see in a moment—heard God speaking through a heavenly voice (Exod. 24). "Now Peter and those who were with him were heavy with sleep but kept awake, and they saw his glory and the two men who stood with him" (Luke 9:32).

What does it mean that Moses and Elijah spoke with Jesus "about his departure"? The Greek word translated here as "departure" (*exodos*) is the same term that the Septuagint uses for the departure of the Hebrews from Egypt, the *Exodus*. In other words, Moses learns (along with Elijah), that Jesus will soon lead an *exodus from bondage* at the Holy City, just as he, himself, once led the Israelites in an exodus from their servitude in Egypt. Not unnaturally, the eavesdropping apostles likely interpreted this news of an exodus solely in terms of literal liberation from the yoke of Rome. Moses knew, however—perhaps better than anyone—that Israel's real troubles began *after* their release from pagan captivity.

Whether in Egypt or in the Promised Land, the Israelites were still sinners; and Moses, for all his inspired leadership, had never been able to break that spiritual yoke. By this point, he would certainly have agreed with the author of Hebrews that "the law has but a shadow of the good things to come instead of the true form of these realities, it can never, by the same sacrifices which are continually offered year after year, make perfect those who draw near . . . For it is impossible that the blood of bulls and goats should take away sins" (Heb. 10:1,4). The Great Jubilee of the Essenes promised a better liberation, from the debt of sin and bondage to the devil . . . but the concept was still, even at this late hour, being confounded with the mere political freedom with which most Israelites might have been content. Moses knew better.

"And as the men were parting from him, Peter said to Jesus, 'Master, it is well that we are here; let us make three booths, one for you and one for Moses and one for Elijah'—not knowing what he said" (Luke 9:33). Preachers who have desired, for whatever reason, to diminish the stature of Peter through the years have often paused to specially emphasize this last, unflattering phrase, "not knowing what he said"—choosing to depict our headstrong working man blurting out the first fool thing that came into his head, without any idea of what he was talking about. In reality, the evangelist is simply establishing that Peter, in his ignorance of God's real plan, is so carried away by the joy of what he is experiencing that he tries to cut straight to the happy ending, to the banquet of intimacy with God and the saints that really is our Lord's ultimate aim in everything he is doing.

"Peter didn't know what he was saying," writes Cyril of Jerusalem, "for before the Savior's passion, resurrection, and victory over death and corruption, it was impossible for Peter to be with Christ and to be permitted into the tents which are in heaven. These things would happen only after the Savior's resurrection and ascent into heaven."[xxii] In calling Peter out for "not knowing what he said," the Evangelist is simply reminding us that there are, alas, some unhappy, un-skippable tasks ahead that must be accomplished first.

Peter's outburst definitely seems less silly when some of the important Jewish backstory is taken into account. What was up with those three booths, anyway? As it happens, the Jews celebrated (and still do celebrate) an actual *feast of booths*, the festival of *Sukkot* commemorating God's presence in the Ark of the Covenant as it traveled through the wilderness along with his people, sheltered every night, as they were, by booths or huts. The Talmud, in fact, refers to this presence as God's *Shekinah*—his willingness to "dwell" or "be sheltered," a word that shares the same Hebrew root behind the word *tabernacle*. Because of this, the Festival of Tents was also known to them as the festival of *Immanuel*—of "God with us." So Peter's often ridiculed proposal actually illustrates something very profound: it shows the apostle's willingness to shelter the man Jesus with a Sukkot booth, just as the ark had been sheltered . . . and for the same reason.

"As [Peter] said this, a cloud came and overshadowed them; and they were afraid as they entered the cloud" (Luke 9:34). If this cloud was, as the Church has believed,[xxiii] that same cloud that often hovered over the Ark of the Covenant while it was within the tabernacle, then the apostles were right to be afraid. "There I will meet with you," God told Moses while giving instructions for the making of the ark, "and from above the mercy seat, from between the two cherubim that are upon the ark of the testimony, I will speak with you of all that I will give you in commandment for the people of Israel" (Exod. 25:22). The mercy seat was the lid of the ark; and the space between the images of the angels was called the *Oracle*, the spot from which the voice of God emanated. "The Lord said to Moses: Tell your brother Aaron not to come at just any time into the sanctuary inside the curtain before the mercy seat that is upon the ark, or he will die; for I appear in the cloud upon the mercy seat" (Lev. 16:2, NRSV). The people came to regard the Oracle as the very dwelling place of God on earth and to identify the cloud with the *Shekinah* itself, the visible token of his special presence. Dozens of Old Testament passages, in fact, speak of Yahweh as "sitting by the cherubim" or "enthroned over" them as, for example, in Psalm 99: "The Lord reigns; let the peoples tremble! He sits enthroned upon the cherubim; let the earth quake!" Little wonder that our Lord's three chosen witnesses, Peter, James, and John, quailed at the thought of being engulfed by it. "And a voice came out of the cloud, saying, 'This is my Son, my Chosen; listen to him!' And when the voice had spoken, Jesus was found alone" (Luke 9:34-35).

Here is probably our best proof that Peter was praised by Christ for being the first to glimpse the implications of his Sonship in their fullness. His inchoate urge to worship, displayed—in however inappropriate a form—here at the Transfiguration, proves that Peter has reached the conclusion that his great Instructor has been seeking to inculcate all along: that God "dwells inside" the man Jesus, just as the

Shekinah of God once dwelt inside the ark.[50] "Moses was there, and Elijah," adds St. Augustine; "The voice did not say: These are my beloved *sons*. For one only is the Son; others are adopted. It is he that is commended to them: He from whom the law and prophets derive their glory."[xxiv] Jesus, as Chrysostom concludes, "disclosed a glimpse of the Godhead" at the Transfiguration. "He manifested to them the God who was dwelling among them."[xxv]

Yet nine of the twelve, remember, had not made the cut, were not allowed to be present at the Transfiguration. And worse than that, our Lord did not even permit those who *had* been present to tell anyone about it—not even, it would seem, the other apostles! "As they were coming down the mountain, he ordered them to tell no one about what they had seen, until after the Son of Man had risen from the dead. So they kept the matter to themselves, questioning what this rising from the dead could mean" (Mark 9:10). Luke's version doubles down on this, making it clear that this temporary embargo really was strictly observed for the entirety of the prescribed period: "And they kept silent and in those days told no one any of the things they had seen" (Luke 9:36). What was the thinking behind this?

Several of the early Fathers ventured to guess that our Lord was concerned his less-mature disciples might take the Transfiguration as a sign that *the kingdom had already come*, or that his victory was now such a foregone conclusion that further work and prayers on their part would be superfluous.

50 This phraseology might seem slightly dicey in terms of our later, developed Christological dogmas about the hypostatic union and the Incarnation of the Son . . . if our Savior hadn't used it himself at the Last Supper: "Do you not believe that I am in the Father and the Father in me? The words that I say to you I do not speak on my own authority; but the Father who dwells in me does his works" (John 14:10).

We are never, at any rate, told the reason outright in Scripture. We can only assume that master Teacher, in his infinite wisdom, simply knew that these others needed to grasp the Great Mystery in some other way. It is perfectly certain, however, that the tone of his teaching changes from about this point forward; the "minor key" kicks in now, and it becomes the dominant tenor until the embargo is lifted—"until after the Son of Man had risen from the dead." And Peter, James, and John, God bless them, move smoothly on to their next task at hand: "questioning," that is, "what this rising from the dead could mean."

It seems perfectly obvious to us, of course, with our 20/20 hindsight. The words, after all, are quite literal and unadorned: "Then he began to teach them that the Son of Man must undergo great suffering, and be rejected by the elders, the chief priests, and the scribes, and be killed, and after three days rise again. He said all this quite openly" (Mark 8:31-32). He said it so openly, in fact, that he appears to grow impatient at their dullness after a while. During another miracle of deliverance, "while everyone was amazed at all that he was doing, he said to his disciples, 'Let these words sink into your ears: The Son of Man is going to be betrayed into human hands.' But they did not understand this saying; its meaning was concealed from them, so that they could not perceive it. And they were afraid to ask him about this saying" (Luke 9:44-45).

Why couldn't they perceive it? What—beyond the obvious fact that a divine being cannot die—was hindering their understanding?

Many theories have been offered through the years. Perhaps the apostles wondered if it was just another of the master's impenetrable parables (of which there really had, to be fair, been more than a few so far); or possibly they took it as some kind of metaphor about the rise and fall and rising again of the nation itself. But the best explanation, it would seem, lies in an understanding of the psychology of *preconceived notions*—of the power of expectations and the cognitive dissonance that occurs when expectations are too abruptly thwarted. We've taken more than one opportunity in these pages to fault those for whom the idea of a coming Messiah was valued chiefly as a solution to this-worldly problems; those Jews who, given a Prince of Prince, might have been just as happy with another snarling Samson, hacking away at the nasty foreigners with the jawbone of an ass.

But the truth is, the appearance of contradiction we noted while sketching the hopes of Nathanael—the vexing paradox of *Suffering Savior vs. Military Messiah*—cannot be easily waved away. The drumbeat of war is simply too recurrent a theme in Old Testament prophecy; and, uncomfortable as it may be for many of us to realize, that note sounds in those sacred pages at least as often as the "Man of Sorrows" motif, if not more often.

"I see him, but not now," prophecies Moses; "I behold him, but not near—a star shall come out of Jacob, and a scepter shall rise out of Israel; it shall crush the borderlands of Moab, and the territory of all the Shethites" (Num. 24:17).

"Give the king your justice, O God," implores Solomon, "and your righteousness to a king's son . . . May he defend the cause of the poor of the people, give deliverance to the needy, and crush the oppressor. May his foes bow down before him, and his enemies lick the dust . . . For he delivers the needy when they call, the poor and those who have no helper . . . From oppression and violence he redeems their life; and precious is their blood in his sight" (Ps. 72:1, 4-5, 12, 14).

"The Lord says to my lord," writes David, "'Sit at my right hand until I make your enemies your footstool.' The

Lord sends out from Zion your mighty scepter. Rule in the midst of your foes. Your people will offer themselves willingly on the day you lead your forces on the holy mountains . . . The Lord is at your right hand; he will shatter kings on the day of his wrath. He will execute judgment among the nations, filling them with corpses; he will shatter heads over the wide earth" (Ps. 110:1-3, 5-6).

So why was Jesus' talk of failure so difficult to comprehend? Surely it was because so many of the ancient prophecies appeared to demand success! "For the days are surely coming," writes Jeremiah the prophet, "when I will restore the fortunes of my people, Israel and Judah, says the Lord, and I will bring them back to the land that I gave to their ancestors and they shall take possession of it. . . . On that day, says the Lord of hosts, I will break the yoke from off his neck, and I will burst his bonds, and strangers shall no more make a servant of him. But they shall serve the Lord their God and David their king, whom I will raise up for them" (Jer. 30:7-9).[51] Yet, this element of *vindication* seemed missing in Jesus' ministry thus far. Yes, he showed all the expected signs otherwise . . . but where was the victory? The story made no sense without the happy ending; and the new ending Jesus appeared to be insisting on seemed, well, a let-down to say the least. And there are reasons to guess that, for at least three of our Lord's later recruits, the puzzle became a make-or-break crisis that threatened to send them away into the wilderness from which they had come.

According to Origen, Simon the Zealot (the Simon, that is, who did not become Peter) received his call to apostleship along with Andrew, Peter, and Philip along the shores of Tiberias in Galilee. This area may have had a great many

51 David, it should be noted, had been dead nearly 500 years when Jeremiah wrote these words.

Essenes, yet it was also the headquarters of a similar but much earthier group of revolutionaries: the party of the Zealots.[52]

Dissatisfied, like their cousins, with the way the Pharisees went about their business, the Zealots differed dramatically from the Essenes in their militancy, their "by any means necessary" attitude toward driving out the hated Roman occupiers. Along the way, they gave their name to the English language as a word for any group of blind, unreasoning fanatics; an association they earned through their suicidal devotion to the cause and their many gruesome acts of terrorism. Like the Essenes, the Zealots looked for a Messiah who would resurrect the old Davidic monarchy and then act as recognized head on earth of all twelve original tribes of Israel. It was likely this expectation that first drew Simon (perhaps by way of John the Baptist) into the circle of the Nazarene.

Probably he got a good deal more than he was bargaining for, including (as we have seen) the power to work miracles in Jesus' name! Simon may started out with purely political considerations in mind but his willingness to stay this long—right up until the cusp of the Exodus—certainly indicates that he cannot have been a typical Zealot. He was surely a Zealot on a journey. His willingness to listen to so much preaching about peace and forgiveness, about turning the other cheek and putting one's hopes on heaven rather than earth, proves the distance he had already traveled. But

52 This Simon is surnamed *Kananaios* in Matthew's Gospel (which led St. Jerome to mistakenly identify him as a Canaanite) but Luke and Acts call him *Zelotes*; both words are renderings of the same Hebrew root *qana*, meaning "the zealous one." Scripture doesn't actually say that Simon was or had been associated with the political party of the Zealots but the name of that party—very much "in the news" at the time—is also derived from *qana*.

all this new talk of rejection, death, and betrayal from the master may have triggered a critical decision point.

If we cheat and use our foreknowledge of things to come, as Simon couldn't, we may see how striking were the stakes. The murderer Barabbas, later preferred by the Jerusalemites to our Lord, was a Zealot—possibly one of Simon's old co-conspirators; his name remains a symbol of folly and the fickleness of mobs to this very day. Afterward, the Zealots led the entire nation to complete ruin by a very short path. Instrumental in arranging the violent uprising of A.D. 70, they became so enraged by what they saw as the timidity and compromises of their less-zealous countrymen that they ended by turning their swords more savagely on their fellow Jews than on the Romans. The result was the defilement and total destruction of the Temple to which they avowed such devotion and, according to Josephus the historian, literal rivers of Jewish blood in the streets of the Holy City. Their last stand at the fortress of Masada a year or so later pretty much finished the party of the Zealots for good; terminating, as it did, in a grotesque suicide pact among the final die-hards that left the Roman conquerors, who finally did breach the walls, with nothing on their hands but a heap of corpses, many of them women and children.

Without knowing it, this was the future with which Simon the Zealot was gambling as he pondered whether or not to give up on a Messiah who seemed increasingly reconciled to a fatalistic finale for his own career.

Exacerbating Simon the Zealot's difficulties may have been the continued presence of Matthew/Levi in the apostolic band, the former quisling and collaborator. "Is it not amazing," asks Evangelical scholar Herbert Lockyer, "to place two of these members in the band together . . . the religious puritan and the social pariah . . . the tax gatherer and the tax-hater side by side? . . . Simon had been a Jewish patriot chafing under a foreign yoke, sighing for emancipation. Matthew was an unpatriotic Jew who degraded himself by becoming an agent of the Roman rulers, whom Simon sought to destroy."[xxvi] Matthew, too, had clearly been on some kind of a journey but probably had not, any more than Simon, completely outgrown his former attitudes and prejudices. Probably there were periodic flareups between them, not dissimilar to those experienced nowadays at holiday gatherings, where political disagreements lying just under the surface threaten to erupt and overcome the deeper family ties.

These two may simply have gotten on each other's nerves. Some scholars believe that Matthew may have been the best educated and perhaps, before his call, the most worldly of the apostles. His occupation required literacy and facility with numbers. From his constant contact with the wealthy and the urbane from whom he collected taxes, he likely acquired an ability to thrive in their milieu, with a veneer of sophistication that would have been highly irritating to an impatient idealist such as Simon. And if Matthew did experience any temptation as this new note of fatalism entered his master's voice, it could have sprung from just this source. He had demonstrated a characteristically Jewish talent for making peace with despair once already. Having overcome every scruple in order to take up the very worst job a Hebrew could do in the eyes of his countrymen, he had already proven himself a man who could survive the complete loss of any hope or idealism. Was he, by this point, already triangulating his exit and (perhaps semi-consciously) formulating a backup plan for life in the new post-Jesus reality?

And then, not least, there was Judas of Kerioth—the

twelfth man.[53] Kerioth was a small village a few miles south of Hebron; thus Judas was a Judean, not a Galilean like the other eleven. Those of us who know what eventually came of Judas (that is, pretty much the whole world) might be tempted to guess that he was deliberately chosen to be an outsider at odds with his brethren—"the alien apostle" as one writer has put it. Jesus' own statement—"Did I not choose you, the twelve? Yet one of you is a devil" (John 6:70)—might be taken as verification that Judas never had any chance of turning out properly to begin with.

The Church, however, has never seen Christ's foreknowledge as grounds for believing that any given individual is ever damned without his conscious participation. St. Cyril of Alexandria points out, for instance, that Jesus did not actually finger Judas publicly by that statement: "For he does not say clearly who shall betray him, but rather, by laying the burden of iniquity on one of the disciples, without saying whom, Jesus brought them all to the contest. And so, with each one dreading the loss of his own soul, Jesus invites them to more careful circumspection."[xxvii] If we were to suppose, as Catholic scholar William H. Kent points out, that Judas "never really believed, if he was a false disciple from the first, or, as the apocryphal Arabic Gospel of the Infancy has it, was possessed by Satan even in his childhood, then he would not have felt the holy influence of Christ or enjoyed the light and spiritual gifts of the apostolate."[xxviii]

It could be that Judas was simply the first among the twelve to take Jesus' prophecies of earthy failure literally. If, like Simon the Zealot, Judas originally hitched his wagon to Jesus' star in hopes of helping to bring about a political

53 "Iscariot" is a Greek version of the Hebrew phrase "a man of Kerioth" or Carioth, which was a town in Judah (cf. Josh. 15:25).

revolution, then he may have been quicker than the others in detecting, from the many hints in the Nazarene's own teaching, that those hopes were not going to be literally fulfilled anytime soon. Simon may have been the purer patriot, with a genuinely selfless desire to see his nation revived; Judas, on the other hand, might simply have lost interest when his dreams of an important post in the new order (dreams which, to be fair, he shared with Peter, James, and John) began to fade. By the time Simon, Matthew, and the rest had reached the same conclusions, they must have realized that they had developed a personal attachment to their master quite apart from any program. But Judas may have felt he'd been made a fool of, sold a bill of goods; possibly even believed that Jesus, with all his talk of thrones and kingdoms to come and the crown of David, had consciously misrepresented himself to his prospects. At that, a less conflicted man would, of course, have felt duty-bound to resign his exalted post, to confess that he no longer had enough confidence in the enterprise to hold his position in good faith. Judas chose to linger instead, retaining his job with the thought, perhaps, of scouting out some way to yet salvage an advantage from his association with so famous a personality.

These, at any rate, may have been something like the temptations of the doubtful as Jesus' prophesied exodus began.

Jesus and his apostles entered Jerusalem to carry away the captives of Belial on the first day of Passover week—just as the original Exodus began with Passover. This epoch-changing event had been visualized by the Israelite prophets for centuries: Messiah comes to the Holy City at last. "When he had come near Bethphage and Bethany," two small towns at the entrance to the Holy City proper,

> at the place called the Mount of Olives, he sent two of the disciples, saying, "Go into the village

> ahead of you, and as you enter it you will find tied there a colt that has never been ridden. Untie it and bring it here. If anyone asks you, "Why are you untying it?" just say this, "The Lord needs it." So those who were sent departed and found it as he had told them. As they were untying the colt, its owners asked them, "Why are you untying the colt?" They said, "The Lord needs it." Then they brought it to Jesus; and after throwing their cloaks on the colt, they set Jesus on it (Luke 19:29-35).

Here, Matthew's Gospel interrupts us for a moment to point out something: "This took place to fulfill what had been spoken through the prophet [Zechariah], saying, 'Tell the daughter of Zion, Look, your king is coming to you, humble, mounted on a donkey, on a colt, the foal of a donkey'" (21:5). Interestingly, however, Zechariah himself had definitely appeared to connect this idea with the Military Messiah rather than the Suffering Savior. Here is how his more complete statement reads:

> [In those days] I will encamp at my house as a guard, so that no one shall march to and fro; no oppressor shall again overrun them, for now I have seen with my own eyes. Rejoice greatly, O daughter Zion! Shout aloud, O daughter Jerusalem! Lo, your king comes to you; triumphant and victorious is he, humble and riding on a donkey, on a colt, the foal of a donkey. He will cut off the chariot from Ephraim and the war horse from Jerusalem; and the battle bow shall be cut off, and he shall command peace to the nations; his dominion shall be from sea to sea (Zech. 9:8-10).

Notice the strange mixing of metaphors in this passage. The king rides on a humble donkey, not a war horse. And yet here the humble man on the foal of an ass is going to (1) free Zion from her oppressors, (2) drive out the chariots of Ephraim (the northern tribes of the Ephraimites who by Zechariah's day had become Judah's enemy), (3) stop attackers who came with battle-bows, and (4) dictate peace terms to the nations (to the pagan Gentiles, that is). Afterward, he will have a "dominion"—a place where he will act as *Dominus* (Lord). The apostles (including Matthew/Levi, the very author who steps in to make sure we won't miss Zechariah's paradox) are beginning to grasp, it seems, the outline of an exceptionally difficult conception.

The Man on the Donkey . . . and the Conquering King who will cut off the war horse . . . must be one and the same. It's not an either/or proposition—it's an antinomy. Both things are true, but maybe *not both things at once.*

7

A CHANGE OF PRIESTHOOD

"For when there is a change in the priesthood, there is necessarily a change in the law as well."

—Hebrews 7:12

The story of our Lord's sorrowful passion—the saving events that took place at Jerusalem during the pivotal week in human history—has been told often, by the greatest writers of our civilization. Our purpose here is not to retell them again but to revisit them rather narrowly, pausing only over what directly affected the founding of the Apostolic College and what may illumine Christ's purposes in establishing it.

Jesus' public ministry ended on Tuesday afternoon of Passion Week. After managing one final round of traps from the Pharisees and the Sadducees, our Lord entered a kind of lockdown mode, in fulfillment of Isaiah's long-ago prophecy: "He was oppressed, and he was afflicted, yet he did not open his mouth; like a lamb that is led to the slaughter, and like a sheep that before its shearers is silent, so he did not open his mouth" (Isa. 53:7). After this he would speak (besides a few short words to his judges during his trials) only to the twelve apostles. And the rest of his talk will be focused almost entirely on making the final arrangements for looking after, in his absence, the Church he had promised to build—and continuing its work after his departure.

First then, the bad news: Jesus is leaving—for a short while to begin with, afterward for a more extended period. "Little children, I am with you only a little longer. You will look for me; and as I said to the Jews so now I say to you, 'Where I am going, you cannot come" (John 8:21). So, Jesus is prepping *stand-ins*; pinch-hitters, proxies, ambassadors. The ancient churches have used the word *vicars*: someone empowered to act on another's behalf. And in these last few days before the parting, "Jesus is clearly assigning the twelve as his vicars," according to Catholic scholar Scott Hahn. "He is telling them that he will act vicariously through them."[xxix] In short, he had created miracle men like himself to leave behind . . . because he knew he would not be present on earth to establish the Church in person.

One of the reasons this fact has been unclear to many through the centuries is that preachers and Christian writers have so often chosen to emphasize only one side of what is very much a two-sided equation. Yes, Christ promised to remain with us always, to the end of the age (Matt. 28:20). And yes, St. Paul writes to the Christians at Colossae, of "Christ in you, the hope of glory" (Col. 1:27). Yet this is the same. Paul who longs so much to see Jesus again in person that he confesses to the Philippians of being torn between two choices: "For to me, living is Christ and dying is gain. If I am to live in the flesh, that means fruitful labor for me; and I do not know which I prefer. I am hard pressed between the two: my desire is to depart and be with Christ, for that is far better; but to remain in the flesh is more necessary for you" (Phil. 1:21-24). The Church has walked this same tightrope through the centuries; acknowledging his spiritual presence among us without denying our longing for immediate fellowship with him as a man among men.

This is why the most characteristic attitude of the Christian has not been a mere stoic acceptance of his will—"It is to your advantage that I go away" (John 16:17)—but, rather, that cry of the heart we find at the very end of the Bible, at the conclusion of St. John's Apocalypse: *Maranatha!*—Come, Lord Jesus! *The Spirit and the Bride say, "Come!"* We have been (to employ another humble metaphor) like tow-headed Brandon de Wilde at the end of the classic film, standing bereft at the edge of the farmstead, piteously calling out *"Shane! Come back, Shane!"* as Alan Ladd rides slowly and sadly into the sunset. We speak, quite properly, of his Real Presence in the sacrament of the altar (and in other important senses) but we falsify a key element of our unbroken Tradition if we deny in practice his equally real *absence*. By allowing ourselves to emphasize too exclusively the spiritual comforts we do enjoy, we have at times made the need for any kind of earthly management (through this principle of vicarage) seem superfluous.

There's no doubt at all, however, that Jesus really did intend to leave someone in charge. Even before the final round of commissionings that we will consider here at the Passion, his will in this matter had been made perfectly clear. On the same occasion when told his disciples, "Behold, I have given you authority to tread upon serpents and scorpions, and over all the power of the enemy," (Luke 10:19), he also "rejoiced in the Holy Spirit and said, 'I thank thee, Father, Lord of heaven and earth, that thou hast hidden these things from the wise and understanding and revealed them to babes; yea, Father, for such was thy gracious will. All things have been delivered to me by my Father; and no one knows who the Son is except the Father, or who the Father is except the Son and any one to whom the Son chooses to reveal him" (Luke 10:21-22).

Apostleship matters. Jesus is disclosing hitherto unheard-of truths to his disciples—and *only* to them. Afterward, it will be up to them to pass the same truths along to disciples of their own. Commenting on this passage, Tertullian laid out the important conclusion: "If the Lord Jesus Christ sent the apostles to preach, no others ought to be received except those appointed by Christ: for no one knows the Father except the Son, and him to whom the Son gives a revelation. Nor does it seem that the Son has given revelation to any others than the apostles, whom he sent forth to preach what he had revealed to them."[xxx]

Earlier during the same discourse, Our Lord had put the matter as clearly as human speech is capable of doing: "He who hears you hears me, and he who rejects you rejects me, and he who rejects me rejects him who sent me" (Luke 10:16). To tell humanity that it must obey the words of a certain set of men as if they were listening to God himself . . . is a very grave thing to say. This kind of mission from Jesus would, by its very nature, require a special *power* from Jesus as well; it implies that the apostles have been given some kind of miraculous gift that will protect them from speaking falsehood, with Christ's own sanction, to the world in the name of God. Here St. Cyril of Alexandria switches over to Matthew's account: "Christ himself said to the holy disciples, 'For it is not you that speak, but the Spirit of your Father speaking through you.' Christ speaks in them by the same consubstantial Spirit" (10:19).[xxxi] This thought will later be reflected as the Church comes to recognize that the books and letters written by the apostles (or under their auspices) can be trusted as *an inerrant word from God,* not just another word of man—in other words, as Scripture.

The apostles bring their extensive training in the

all-important subject of God's kingdom all the way to the final week. That Jesus, at his Roman trial, told Pilate, "My kingdom is not of this world" (John 18:36), would not have implied to them that the kingdom they had heard so much about was not a real society with a real constitution, real laws, and real officers. They had been made to understand that Christ's is a kingdom *in* the world but not *of* the world.[54] Jesus prays for them in just these terms as his exodus draws near: "I have given them thy word; and the world has hated them because they are not of the world, even as I am not of the world. I do not pray that thou shouldst take them out of the world, but that thou shouldst keep them from the evil one. They are not of the world, even as I am not of the world" (John 17:14-17). The twelve *knew* that the kingdom of God was a genuine society, for they had been living in it—in an embryonic form—for the prior three glorious years. They knew if was solid enough to have been compared to a house built on rock, a light that cannot be hidden, and the eventual basis of fellowship between all men; with they, themselves, specially empowered to organize it.

In the Upper Room, on the night Jesus was betrayed, the twelve apostles learned that Christ's kingdom was to have its own *set form of worship*, as well; its own liturgical rituals, its own sacrifice, its own priesthood, just as God had formerly given to the Temple—new in one sense, but also very ancient. We have seen how Jesus defended the actions of his apostles in the matter of the grain gathered and eaten on the Sabbath by showing David and his men acting as priests—though not, clearly, of the Levitical variety. This parallelism implies, of course, that Jesus and his apostles were, or soon would be, acting in the same capacity. Yet the Levites were

54 The same verse, in fact, in which Jesus disclaims a kingdom "of this world," ends with a clarification: "My kingship is not from this world" (John 18:36).

the one and only set of priests sanctioned by Moses' law; to find any other priesthood in the pages of the Old Testament, we must go back to the time prior to Moses' law, to the age of the patriarchs—and look, if possible, to find *priests before the priests*. And if we do this, we come quickly to Genesis 14, where the mysterious notices of Melchizedek first appear.

In that chapter, Abraham rescues his nephew Lot from captivity to the five kings who had defeated his people at the Valley of Siddim. Upon his return, the patriarch receives a blessing from a figure about whom almost nothing else is known for certain outside of verse 18: "And Melchizedek king of Salem brought out bread and wine; he was priest of God Most High." Abraham lived about 500 years before Moses; so here is a priest, offering the same sacrificial elements we see Christ himself offering at the Last Supper, long before the Levitical priesthood was ever minted, with its sacrifices of blood and grain. Then, many centuries later, during an era when Moses' law had been operative for close to 300 years, we find David composing a psalm that Christ himself will later identify as a prophecy of Messiah (Luke 20:41-44): "The LORD says to my lord: 'Sit at my right hand, till I make your enemies your footstool' . . . The LORD has sworn and will not change his mind, 'You are a priest for ever after the order of Melchizedek'" (Psalm 110:1, 4). Jesus *is* a priest, then—as his actions at the grain field indicated—distinct from that established by Moses and Aaron.

Did Melchizedek's order pass away when the covenant made at Sinai went into effect? Apparently not, since the man Jesus can take up its rites and privileges again. "Genesis implies," according to commentators Scott Hahn and Curtis Mitch, "that the order of Melchizedek is the patriarchal order of priesthood that functioned for many centuries before the ordination of Aaron and his sons took place at Mt. Sinai [Lev 8:1-36]."[xxxii] Extrabiblical Jewish sources (such as the Talmud and Targums) sometimes linked Melchizedek to the patriarchs very directly indeed; several of them identify Melchizedek with Noah's righteous son Shem, ascribing to him a Methuselah-like longevity that allowed him to live long enough to bless Abraham in his day!

Be that as it may, throughout the book of Genesis we certainly see the patriarchs performing all the characteristic functions of a priest: building altars, consecrating shrines, pouring out thank offerings, and offering sacrifice on behalf of God's family. This was the original, pre-Levitical form of priesthood that existed before Moses' law ever came into being. The priesthood which Jesus takes up, then, isn't so much a new one as the reemergence of a priesthood *temporarily suspended.* As the author of the book of Hebrews writes: "Christ did not exalt himself to be made a high priest, but was appointed by him who said to him . . . 'You are a priest for ever, according to the order of Melchizedek'" (Heb. 5:5–6).

"Now if perfection had been attainable through the Levitical priesthood," we are asked in Hebrews 7,

> What further need would there have been for another priest to arise after the order of Melchizedek, rather than one named after the order of Aaron? For when there is a change in the priesthood, there is necessarily a change in the law as well . . . On the one hand, a former commandment is set aside because of its weakness and uselessness (for the law made nothing perfect); on the other hand, a better hope is introduced, through which we draw near to God. This makes Jesus the surety of a better covenant (Heb. 7:22).

"Insofar as Psalm 110:4 envisions a change from the Levitical priesthood of Aaron to the Melchizedekian priesthood of Christ," according to Hahn and Mitch, "it follows that Mosaic laws of worship must also give way to the messianic laws of worship."

Practically all Christians accept the Melchizedek priesthood exercised by Jesus himself. Some movements, however, have marshaled arguments against the tradition that Jesus ordained any additional priests to minister in the Church during his absence. They often cite 1 Peter 2:9, in which the fisherman addresses the faithful as "a chosen race, a royal priesthood, a holy nation, God's own people." This verse is held to illustrate the existence of a *priesthood of all believers* that has superseded and obviated the need for any sort of ministerial priesthood such as the Jews possessed.

This, though, is surely the argument that proves too much, since Peter is echoing the words of Exodus 19:6! Yes, even Old Covenant Israel had been a kingdom of priests, just as ancient Christianity has always recognized the Church to be. Israel had both a common priesthood in which all the faithful participated . . . *and* a ministerial priesthood of Levites. Christ, as we are about to see, envisioned no change to this pattern but rather merely renovated the priesthood to its former condition, when Melchizidek "brought out bread and wine"—before the regular sacrifice of bulls and goats was mandated for a period instead.[55]

The apostles didn't so much replace the Levitical priests as step back in, thank them for their service and for holding the fort during a difficult stretch, and then allow them to enjoy a long-deserved Sabbath rest. Gathered together in the

55 "The whole Church is a priestly people. Through baptism all the faithful share in the priesthood of Christ. This participation is called the 'common priesthood of all the faithful.' Based on this common priesthood and ordered to its service, there exists another participation in the mission of Christ: the ministry conferred by the sacrament of holy orders, where the task is to serve in the name and in the person of Christ the head in the midst of the community" (CCC 1591).

Cenacle, they watched as Jesus began to perform a series of acts in front of them that were both strange . . . and strangely familiar:

> And when the hour came, he sat at table, and the apostles with him. And he said to them, "I have earnestly desired to eat this Passover with you before I suffer; for I tell you I shall not eat it until it is fulfilled in the kingdom of God." And he took a cup, and when he had given thanks he said, "Take this, and divide it among yourselves; for I tell you that from now on I shall not drink of the fruit of the vine until the kingdom of God comes." And he took bread, and when he had given thanks he broke it and gave it to them, saying, "This is my body which is given for you. Do this in remembrance of me." And likewise the cup after supper, saying, "This cup which is poured out for you is the new covenant in my blood" (Luke 22:14-20).

The Passover had been the sacred meal of the Hebrews, commemorating the night when a mark of blood made on the doorposts of the faithful (a mark, according to tradition, inscribed in the form of an X-shaped cross) caused the death angel to pass them over during the final plague before the Exodus. Here, Jesus is telling his men that this will be the last of the old Passovers—the last *anticipatory* Passover, that is. What did Jesus mean when he said, "I shall not eat it again until it is fulfilled in the kingdom of God" (a saying that echoes his previous words in Matthew 5:18 that the whole Law of Moses would pass away once it had been "fulfilled")?

Medieval exegete Robert Grossteste explains this language:

> To fulfill . . . and not destroy a thing whose existence is transient is to lead it through its natural progression continually unto its end . . . For example: to fulfill and not destroy the seed of a tree or the seed of grain is to cause it to die by decaying in soil and through germination to pass into a tree or an ear of grain, and so to cease to have the form and existence of the seed. Therefore, he fulfills and does not destroy a seed who in the aforementioned way brings the seed to non-existence, because the true existence of the seed is to pass in this manner into non-existence. But he who hides a seed in a storeroom and keeps it for many years and does not allow it to germinate by dying and does not allow something more imperfect to pass away by dying and germinating—he who does this truly destroys the seed and ruins it.[xxxiii]

This is a sense in which the old Passover—which Moses commanded to be done—passed away but was not destroyed. It was *transformed* instead . . . and the apostles gradually became aware that they were watching it happen before their eyes.

John's Gospel includes the story of Jesus washing the feet of his disciples just before this supper. Priests of the Old Covenant had to wash their feet before coming into the Temple to offer the sacrifice of a lamb—something Nathanael, at least (the canon lawyer), would have been very aware of. Now, the apostles hear Jesus "giving thanks" for the bread and the wine. The original Greek word in these verses is *eucharisteo*—an offering of thanks, a "sacrifice of praise" (Heb. 13:15). They hear him speak about *giving his body*, as the sacrificial lamb had given its body under the Old Covenant as an atonement for sins—a powerful reminder, to former disciples of the Baptizer, that Jesus himself had previously been identified to them as "the Lamb of God who takes away the sins of the world" (John 1:29).

The apostles also hear that Jesus' blood is to be "poured out"—a coined phrase used by the Old Testament priests for their own (insufficient) act of atonement in emptying the blood of animal sacrifices at the base of the Temple altar. Most significantly, they hear that Melchizidek's old elements of bread and wine are now, in some sense, *becoming* Christ's body and his blood: "*This* is my body . . . *this cup* is the new covenant." An act is being performed: an act of sacrifice, though the apostles may not yet have understood whence these rites (taking place prior to Jesus' death on the cross) were to gain their power. And that act is being *demonstrated in front of them* so that they will remember, in much the same way that a flight attendant gives a demonstration of life-saving measures to be used in case of emergency.

Finally, Jesus—speaking in private to the twelve apostles (or perhaps the eleven by this point; more on that in a moment)—issues a commandment: "Do this in remembrance of me" (Luke 22:9). The Greek verb (*poieo*) translated here as "do" is the same word the Greek Old Testament uses for the offering Moses made while ordaining Aaron and his sons to the Levitical priesthood (Exod. 29:36-41). The apostles knew the Greek Bible very well—and thus Luke and the other evangelists surely did not employ *poieo* here for nothing.

Likewise, the Greek term for "a remembrance" is *anamnesis*—not just a memorial but a ritual act perpetuating a memory. *Anamnesis* is used in the Septuagint (Lev. 24:7) for the offering of frankincense that accompanied the bread sacrificed by fire. Thus "do this in remembrance" has been understood through the ages as Jesus ordaining the apostles to a similar, but purified, priestly service; directing them to continue making this same offering of thanksgiving—of bread and wine—after he is gone.

"You are those who have continued with me in my trials," Jesus continued. "As my Father appointed a kingdom for me, so do I appoint for you that you may eat and drink at my table in my kingdom, and sit on thrones judging the twelve tribes of Israel" (Luke 22:28-30). David was a king, yes, with a throne . . . just as Melchizedek had been king of Salem (the ancient village that had become *Jeru*-Salem by David's time). But God, as we have seen, declared David a priest, too, "after the order of Melchizedek." Theologian John Bergsma explains that "'eating and drinking at the king's table' was a privilege reserved for the king's sons . . . [So] Jesus' words about the apostles sitting on thrones judging the tribes clearly allude to Psalm 122:3-5, which speaks of the thrones where the Davidic princes sat to judge cases." That passage reads, "Jerusalem, built as a city which is bound firmly together, to which the tribes go up, the tribes of the Lord . . . There thrones for judgment were set, the thrones of the house of David." David's sons, who were heirs like their father to Melchizedek's Jerusalem kingship . . . were heirs to his priesthood as well: "David's sons were priests" (2 Sam. 8:18). This is how the apostles, too, were able to become Melchizedek priests, by virtue of their role as the twelve "princes" of Christ's New Covenant.

The apostles Simon the Zealot and Matthew, we are pleased to note, remained to receive this new ordination; Judas Iscariot, alas, had not.[56] The mystery behind his motivations in betraying our Lord will likely never be understood; all the imponderables of the human heart are

56 Most scholars (but not all) agree that Judas had already departed on his traitorous errand before the eucharistic instructions began.

involved, the darkest recesses of lostness. What little Scripture gives us to work with is distressingly banal. It seems that Judas was chosen to manage the group's (no doubt meager) finances and had begun secretly skimming off the top for his own private use.[57] The frequency of the Nazarene's warnings about "lovers of money" and the difficulties involved when camels try to pass through the eye of a needle may have convinced Judas that Jesus was on to him (as, indeed, he almost certainly was) and it appears to have gotten under his skin.

But it all seems an impossibly petty incentive for committing the greatest crime in history. Probably the long pretense involved in the living of such a spectacular double life drove him a little mad . . . and opened the door to the even darker forces Scripture speaks of. As for whether it would even be possible for a man who has done miracles himself via the power of Christ then to turn on his master and bite the hand that was feeding him his daily bread . . . well, we have our Lord's own word on that: "On that day many will say to me, 'Lord, Lord, did we not prophesy in your name, and cast out demons in your name, and do many mighty works in your name?' And then will I declare to them, 'I never knew you; depart from me, you evildoers'" (Matt. 7:22-23).

It is easier to sympathize with the various authorities who rejected him—though not, of course, to such a degree as to leave them blameless.

---

57 "Wealthy women contributed to the maintenance of Christ and his disciples (Luke 8:3), and Judas was made treasurer and administrator of that fund. The very fact that he was given this responsibility proves that the other apostles had faith in his honesty . . . He carried "the bag"—a secular position requiring a good businessman, not necessarily one who was saintly. With his ability in this direction, Judas might have nursed a secret ambition of becoming 'Chancellor of the Exchequer' in the New Kingdom, about which his master preached" (Herbert Lockyer, *All the Apostles of the Bible*, pg. 104).

The final stance taken by the Judean authorities is memorably illumined, we believe, by analogy with a fascinating modern story Pope Benedict XVI tells in his book *Jesus of Nazareth*. There, the pope summarizes the faith journey of a man he deeply admires, a believing Jew and a professor of theology whose "reverence for the Christian faith and his fidelity to Judaism prompted him to seek a dialogue with Jesus." Rabbi Jacob Neusner sent himself, as a thought experiment, on an imaginative journey to the Holy Land of the first century. There, "he listens, he compares, and he speaks with Jesus himself. He is touched by the greatness and the purity of what is said . . . He constantly tries to understand; he is constantly moved by the greatness of Jesus; again and again he talks with him."[xxxiv] Many of the usual charges against the Nazarene he learns to reject as baseless slander; he accepts, for instance, that Jesus, true to his word, did not teach men to "abolish the Law . . . not one jot or tittle" (cf. Matt 5:18). But the rabbi does ultimately conclude that Jesus *added* to it. What did he add? "Himself."

Neusner saw what we saw in chapter 5—that the teaching of Jesus is "Jesus-centric" (catastrophically so, for Neusner). The rabbi cites, for example, the words of Christ to the rich young man in Matthew 19:21: "'If you would be perfect, go, sell all you have and come follow *me*.'" Neusner can only conclude that perfection, "the state of being holy as God is holy (cf. Lev. 19:2, 11:44), as demanded by the Torah, now consists in following Jesus." The rabbi sees this most plainly illustrated, as we did, in the story of the grain field; "the place where the heart of the conflict is laid bare." Jesus and the apostles "may do on the Sabbath what they do because they stand in the place of the priests in the Temple; the holy place has shifted, now being formed by the circle made up of the master and his disciples."

Here, Neusner's internal dialogue comes to a head:

> His noble reserve leads him to put the question to Jesus' disciple, rather than to Jesus himself: 'Is it really so that your master, the Son of Man, is lord of the Sabbath? . . . I ask again—is your master God?' The issue that is really the heart of the debate is thus finally laid bare. Jesus understands himself as the Torah—as the word of God in person. . . . The heart of the Sabbath disputes is the question about the Son of Man—the question about Jesus Christ himself.[xxxv]

In the end, the pope's noble Jew decides not to follow Jesus. Grace continues to pour out on the whole world, of course; but for now, writes Benedict, Rabbi Neusner "remains—as he himself puts it—with the 'eternal Israel' . . . and takes his leave without any rancor."

The figures we see at Jesus' Sanhedrin trial are *not* in Rabbi Neusner's position; not sincere, observant Jews, that is, following the Torah as God gives them light and strength. Jesus has already exposed them as "evildoers" and "hypocrites" who "bind heavy burdens, hard to bear, and lay them on men's shoulders; but they themselves will not move them with their finger" (Matt. 23:4). Yet in their own distorted way, they see the same point Rabbi Neusner saw: that Jesus is demanding to be accepted on his own terms or not at all . . . and his terms simply beggared the imagination. The Sanhedrin indeed *staggered*—as we have seen the apostles themselves doing; as indeed, any thinking person must do when reaching the frontier of the Incarnation.

The difference, however, is that Israel's religious leaders had a position of special responsibility; as Jesus told the people, "The scribes and the Pharisees sit on Moses' seat; so practice and observe whatever they tell you" (Matt. 23:2). These men were supposed to be the *watchers*, specially tasked to be on the lookout for Messiah and ready to alert the nation when he arrived. Being continually fit for this job, as John the Baptist had been fit, was the very essence of their assignment. So their guilt lay not in their inability to work out a difficult theological puzzle but rather in the moral laxity of which Jesus convicts them: their addiction to luxury and prestige and the resulting spiritual lassitude that rendered them unfit for the great hour to which they were called. They chose, instead, to refuse the Sphinx's Riddle, and to interpret the problem of Jesus as a political predicament instead.

The Nazarene, if accepted on the terms he demanded, would simply *take charge* and everything would change. This would undoubtedly bring about civil war in Palestine—which the Romans, of course, would move to extinguish in their old patented style. "So the chief priests and the Pharisees gathered the council, and said, 'What are we to do? For this man performs many signs. If we let him go on thus, every one will believe in him, and the Romans will come and destroy both our holy place and our nation.' But one of them, Caiaphas, who was high priest that year, said to them, 'You know nothing at all; you do not understand that it is expedient for you that one man should die for the people, and that the whole nation should not perish'" (John 11:47-50),[58] Miracles or no, Jesus was a threat to the delicate political order the Sanhedrin had been working so hard to maintain—perhaps even, to their efforts to avert a first-century Holocaust. So they had to allow *realpolitik* to trump religious concerns; and if the decision troubled the more scrupulous members afterward, they were certainly free, if

58 John adds the following commentary: "He did not say this of his own accord, but being high priest that year he prophesied that Jesus should die for the nation, and not for the nation only, but to gather into one the children of God who are scattered abroad" (vv. 51-52).

they liked, to pick up the pieces for their public via whatever theological legerdemain they saw fit to employ.

In this matter, Rome's sins were quite the same. Pilate didn't want unrest in Palestine any more than the Jews did; his position with the emperor depended on it. And he was equally willing to condemn one man as a method of defusing a larger political problem—a man whom Pilate had already confessed with his own mouth to be "faultless" and "just." Both nations, at any rate, will richly merit, by virtue of their actions here at the climax of Passion Week, the cataclysm of judgment Jesus foresees for Judea in the decades ahead. Whole legions of the Roman army will be rendered extinct by what Josephus will dub "the Jewish Wars"; Second Temple Judaism will be destroyed as a religious system; and the Jews will be banished from their homeland for the next thousand years—all because, as the Savior says, "you did not recognize the time of your visitation from God" (Luke 19:44).

These twelve apostles would face their own dark night of the soul when Jesus' trials reached their appointed verdict. "Then Jesus said to them, 'You will all become deserters because of me this night; for it is written, 'I will strike the shepherd, and the sheep of the flock will be scattered'" (Matt. 26:31). When their master was arrested at Gethsemane not much later, Zechariah's dark prophecy for the apostles was fulfilled: "Then all the disciples deserted him and fled" (Matt. 26:56).

Judas had deserted already, of course; his brethren had watched in horror as he led pagan soldiers into the group's cherished garden sanctum of prayer. Now they were ready to join him in that betrayal, though to a somewhat lesser extent. Interestingly, several of the Fathers single out Peter as the worst betrayer among the eleven. According to Chrysostom, Peter had "lifted himself up over the rest, saying, 'Though they all fall away because of you, I will never fall away.' It may be that in some degree his bravado sprang from jealousy. For at supper they had all been talking about which one of them was the greater."[xxxvi]

Still, we can't help wondering again how men who had seen so much, done such mighty miracles themselves in his name, could have abandoned their post when so many lesser men—in foxholes, at the pumps in the belly of *Titanic*, at the World Trade Center—have held fast for lesser causes. Our Nathanael, after all, fled with the others; Nathanael whose faith began with a miracle literally on day one. But Nathanael makes us think again of the fig tree—an image that may yet, in turn, send our thoughts profitably back to another famous tree from Bible history: *the broom tree* under which the great prophet Elijah lay down to die.

That same mighty Elijah who raised the widow's son, who parted the Jordan like Joshua, and so confidently called down fire from heaven on the prophets of Baal, came to his own point of despair in spite of everything. Exhausted by the end of his career, worn out from persecutions and the people's seeming indifference to his message, Elijah lay down under a scraggly broom tree and "asked that he might die: 'It is enough; now, O Lord, take away my life, for I am no better than my ancestors'" (1 Kings 19:4). Even their former master, John the Baptizer—whom Christ acknowledged as spiritual successor to Elijah—had been allowed to reach a similar point. Buried alive in Herod's foul dungeon, the very man who had identified Jesus for the apostles sent a plaintive message asking him, "Are you the one who is to come, or are we to wait for another?" (Luke 7:20). John, too, had not expected the advent of Messiah to be so dark and its consolations so distant. Hope had been withdrawn . . . and faith, almost, it would seem. So the apostles were not the first, despairing of Israel's promised fig tree, to lie down under the broom tree instead.

The Fathers shine some valuable light on how this could be so. "Anyone who questions how the disciples could have fallen away," writes Origen, "after seeing such great signs and wonders and after hearing words of equal power (for the signs and wonders were performed by his words) should realize that Christ wanted to demonstrate through this warning ["You will all become deserters"] that just as 'no one can say Jesus is Lord except by the Holy Spirit' [1 Cor. 12:3], so also no one is able to keep from falling away except by the Holy Spirit . . . [and] 'the Holy Spirit had not yet been given because Jesus had not yet been glorified' [John 7:39]."[xxxvii]

"He teaches us to know," adds Chrysostom, "what the disciples were before the crucifixion and what they did after the crucifixion. For indeed they who were not able so much as to stand their ground when he was crucified, after his death became mighty and stronger than adamant." [59]

These sayings brilliantly enlighten one of the mysterious promises Jesus had made during his farewell discourse in the Upper Room. "It is to your advantage that I go away, for if I do not go away, the Advocate will not come to you; but if I go, I will send him to you" (John 16:7). *If I do not go away, the Holy Spirit will not come.*[60] Why this should be the case, no man can say. We accept this truth solely on Christ's word, based entirely on a few verses from the Gospel of John. But certainly they illustrate one of the main (and sadly

---

59 John Chrysostom, ACCS Matt Ia, pg. 251. Several of the Fathers also express the idea that Christ may have actively withdrawn some of the graces that kept their courage up—so that they would disperse and not be taken captive, thwarting his plan to leave vicars behind to convert the world.

60 Notice that the Holy Spirit must be *sent into* the world, meaning that he had not been here previously (or not, at least, in an ongoing way).

neglected!) purposes of his sacred death. Jesus knows that *the world cannot do without the Holy Spirit* . . . and he is willing to suffer in order to release him from heaven and usher him into our lives.

This departure will allow his twelve vicars to carry away the gifts of the Spirit, just as the exodus of Moses had allowed the twelve tribes to carry away the spoils of Egypt. Our blessed Savior, therefore, bled and died to make one of the fondest dreams of Israel's old seers come true: "Would that all the Lord's people were prophets," Moses had cried, "and that the Lord would put his spirit on them!" (Num. 11:29). The Lord, speaking through Ezekiel, says, "I will sprinkle clean water upon you, and you shall be clean from all your uncleannesses, and from all your idols I will cleanse you. A new heart I will give you, and a new spirit I will put within you; and I will remove from your body the heart of stone and give you a heart of flesh. I will put my spirit within you, and make you follow my statutes and be careful to observe my ordinances" (Ezek. 36:25-27).

"And you shall know that I am the LORD," continues the same prophet, "when I open your graves, and bring you up from your graves, O my people. I will put my spirit within you, and you shall live, and I will place you on your own soil; then you shall know that I, the LORD, have spoken and will act, says the LORD" (Ezek. 37:13-14).

When the Son of Man finally overcame all obstacles and reached his goal at Jerusalem—the cross of Calvary—*exactly one* of the scattered twelve returned and was present to witness the event. This was the beloved disciple, commonly believed to be John bar Zebedee, the brother of James, one of the "Big Three" who had also been present at the Transfiguration. John approached the cross boldly; he was apparently allowed to do so unmolested because his father had been an old friend of the high priest's, with a house in Jerusalem to which Caiaphas had been a frequent visitor (cf. John 18:15-16). Now John was deeply versed in the Septuagint, the Greek Bible we have mentioned so often in these pages; this fact is amply demonstrated by the dozens of quotes from that version he included within the fourth Gospel. This being the case, we can easily imagine that he was thunderstruck as he watched the uncanny parallels to the second chapter of that Bible's book of Wisdom that he saw playing out before his eyes:

> "Let us lie in wait for the righteous man," reasoned the Unrighteous, "because he is inconvenient to us and opposes our actions; he reproaches us for sins against the law, and accuses us of sins against our training. He professes to have knowledge of God, and calls himself a child of the Lord. He became to us a reproof of our thoughts; the very sight of him is a burden to us, because his manner of life is unlike that of others, and his ways are strange. We are considered by him as something base, and he avoids our ways as unclean; he calls the last end of the righteous happy, and boasts that God is his father.
>
> "Let us see if his words are true, and let us test what will happen at the end of his life; for if the righteous man is God's child, he will help him, and will deliver him from the hand of his adversaries. Let us test him with insult and torture, so that we may find out how gentle he is, and make trial of his forbearance. Let us condemn him to a shameful death, for, according to what he says, he will be protected" (vv. 12-20).

As the end approached, John—never having heard the story a thousand times in church as we have—may have longed to see the experiment play out just as the Unrighteous (in the form of his Judean enemies) did. Would the Father of Christ really allow this to happen? Would the divine Christ *actually die*? So many prophecies seemed to cry out to the contrary!

"Of old," wrote Ethan the Ezrahite,[61]

> thou didst speak in a vision to thy faithful one, and say, "I have set the crown upon one who is mighty, I have exalted one chosen from the people. I have found David, my servant; with my holy oil I have anointed him; so that my hand shall ever abide with him, my arm also shall strengthen him. The enemy shall not outwit him, the wicked shall not humble him. I will crush his foes before him and strike down those who hate him. My faithfulness and my steadfast love shall be with him, and in my name shall his horn be exalted. I will set his hand on the sea and his right hand on the rivers. He shall cry to me, 'Thou art my Father, my God, and the rock of my salvation.' And I will make him the first-born, the highest of the kings of the earth. My steadfast love I will keep for him for ever, and my covenant will stand firm for him. I will establish his line for ever and his throne as the days of the heavens" (Psalm 89:19-29).

61 Ethan the Ezrahite is the songwriter-author of Psalm 89. The title of that psalm says it is "a maskil of Ethan the Ezrahite." In addition to Psalm 89, Ethan the Ezrahite is mentioned in 1 Kings 4:31 as a wise man, yet not as wise as King Solomon, who "was wiser than anyone else, including Ethan the Ezrahite." First Chronicles 2:6 gives the added information that Ethan had four brothers and was the son of Zerah (called Mahol in 1 Kings 4:31).

And yet when, about the ninth hour, the anguished Christ cried out with words from a different Psalm, number 22 by our reckoning—"'*Eli, Eli, lama sabachthani?*' that is, 'My God, my God, why hast thou forsaken me?'" (Matt. 27:46)—John would have known that Jesus had found a spot of his own under the broom tree.

8

THE GREATER WORKS

"Truly, truly, I say to you, he who believes in me will also do the works that I do; and greater works than these will he do, because I go to the Father."

—John 14:12

The Nazarene died on the Friday afternoon of Passover week, executed by the Romans as a disturber of the peace at the instigation of Israel's religious tribunal, the Sanhedrin. The verdict of that body had not been unanimous, however, and one of Jesus' supporters there, Joseph of Arimathea, hastily arranged a decent burial for the Savior later that evening in the expensive tomb he had been saving for himself.

Late Sunday afternoon, two other disciples, who seem to have been away from the Holy City during the events of the Passion and had thus heard only sketchy reports second-hand, experienced an uncanny encounter that seemed, at first, more frightening than hopeful. While walking along the road to Emmaus (about seven miles from Jerusalem) "talking and discussing together, Jesus himself drew near and went with them. But their eyes were kept from recognizing him" (Luke 24:15-16). According to St. Mark's version, "he appeared in another form" (16:12)—a notion that only adds to the ghost-story-feeling of the tale. St. Augustine says that Jesus did not want to be recognized just yet, that he prevented them from recognizing him in order to teach a lesson.

> And he said to them, "What is this conversation which you are holding with each other as you walk?' And they stood still, looking sad. Then one of them, named Cleopas, answered him, "Are you the only visitor to Jerusalem who does not know the things that have happened there in these days?" And he said to them, "What things?" And they said to him, "Concerning Jesus of Nazareth, who was a prophet mighty in deed and word before God and all the people, and how our chief priests and rulers delivered him up to be condemned to death, and crucified him. But we had hoped that he was the one to redeem Israel" (Luke 24:17-21).

Take care to notice that neither Cleopas—who may actually have been Jesus' uncle, the brother of his earthly father, St. Joseph—nor the unnamed disciple accompanying him was among the Twelve. Several early authorities tell us that they were from the larger group of seventy that our Lord sent out in Luke 10. Both had heard rumors, it seems, that some of his female disciples in Jerusalem had gone to the tomb to anoint his body but found it missing, the stone having been rolled away. "And he said to them, 'O foolish men, and slow of heart to believe all that the prophets have spoken! Was it not necessary that the Christ should suffer these things and enter into his glory?' And beginning with Moses and all the prophets, he interpreted to them in all the scriptures the things concerning himself" (Luke 24:27).

The Emmaus Road disciples "had hoped" that Jesus was the one to redeem Israel, but the unhappy ending has shaken their faith. One can almost hear their sigh as they contemplate getting up Monday morning to start, as the poor Baptizer had done under his broom tree, "looking for another."[62] Conditional disciples "hoped" Jesus might be the redeemer; true faith would have *known* that he was, execution or no execution—just as Abraham, when told that the son through whom he had been promised a multitude of descendants, his as-yet-childless son Isaac, would have to be sacrificed on a pyre, took him there in faith having "considered that God was able to raise men even from the dead" (Heb. 11:19). Happily, the Risen Christ had just the prescription for their malady.

He joined them at their lodgings and sat down to a meal. "When he was at table with them, he took the bread and blessed, and broke it, and gave it to them" (Luke 24:30). There was that distinctive phraseology again: *he took, he blessed, he broke, he gave*—the same sequence of words employed not only at the Last Supper but at the Feeding of the Five Thousand (Matt. 14:19), where his lordship over the laws of physics transformed a small amount of normal food into sustenance for a multitude (leaving, it should be noted, twelve basketsful over afterward, another not-coincidental number). Here, in other words, the same Priest who said the

62 Jesus, it should be noted, was very patient with the doubts of his precursor as well. The months of imprisonment and anxiety had taken their toll; the Baptizer finally gave vent to the anguish of the flesh. Our Lord had this to say in response to the embarrassing report: Was John a prophet? "Yes, I tell you, and more than a prophet . . . among those born of women none is greater than John; yet he who is least in the kingdom of God is greater than he" (Luke 7:26, 28).

first eucharistic liturgy in the Cenacle says the second—a "home Mass" so to speak—to a very small congregation at Emmaus. "And their eyes were opened and they recognized him; and he vanished out of their sight" (24:31). A few verses later, these two would reach their destination, where they informed the Eleven about "what had happened on the road, and how he was known to them in the breaking of the bread" (24:35).

They had been hoping he would redeem Israel—but now they *know* that he *has* redeemed it, and by the very acts which they had been reading as failure! When he was interpreting to them in the Scriptures "all the things concerning himself," Jesus must have lingered carefully over Isaiah chapter 53, in which the great prophet had very obviously seen the whole thing coming. Writing as if he were the personification of the entire nation, Isaiah prophesied:

> He was despised and rejected by men; a man of sorrows, and acquainted with grief; and as one from whom men hide their faces he was despised, and we esteemed him not. Surely he has borne our griefs and carried our sorrows; yet we esteemed him stricken, smitten by God, and afflicted. But he was wounded for our transgressions, he was bruised for our iniquities; upon him was the chastisement that made us whole, and with his stripes we are healed. All we like sheep have gone astray; we have turned every one to his own way; and the Lord has laid on him the iniquity of us all . . . And they made his grave with the wicked and with a rich man in his death, although he had done no violence, and there was no deceit in his mouth. Yet it was the will of the Lord to bruise him; he has put him

> to grief; when he makes himself an offering for sin, he shall see his offspring, he shall prolong his days; the will of the Lord shall prosper in his hand; he shall see the fruit of the travail of his soul and be satisfied (53:3-6, 9-11a).

To many critics in the centuries since, the imagery in Isaiah 53 has seemed too detailed, too specific to Christian theology to possibly be authentic; Skeptics in the eighteenth and nineteenth centuries used to wonder if the text might have been tampered with to add these Christian-sounding details after the fact. We say they *used to* wonder . . . because the discovery of the Great Isaiah Scroll in one of the Dead Sea jars changed everything. That scroll—since 1946, the oldest complete example of any biblical book ever found—was copied out (probably by the Essenes) at least a hundred years *before* Christ . . . and it contains chapter 53 word for word as we have it today. But for Jesus' disciples, looking backward, it had been the *sacramental meal* that did the trick—switching on the lights, allowing everything to snap suddenly into place. "They said to each other, 'Did not our hearts burn within us while he talked to us on the road, while he opened to us the scriptures?'" (Luke 24:32).

Yet . . . the "Man of Sufferings" hadn't really been the difficult part to imagine, had it? What had been so troublesome was how the same Man of Sufferings could also be the Man of War, the man bringing vindication and—dare we say it?—vengeance. It took a few more developments to bring to light the solution to that old puzzle, the first of which was to be Christ's unexpected ascension. His exodus had, apparently, not been quite completed at the cross.

Unexpected? Yes, *we* expect it, of course, having grown up with the story. But hadn't our Lord also spoken of it well in advance? Hadn't he told his disciples that the descent of the Spirit depended upon his going away? When they murmured during his Bread of Life discourse (John 6), had he not responded by saying, "Do you take offense at this? Then what if you were to see the Son of man ascending where he was before?" (John 6:62). Yes, he had said these things . . . but then again, he'd alerted them to the Resurrection well in advance, too, and his students apparently waved it away as a metaphor.

Easter morning, at any rate, found the apostles huddled together in despair; in fact, when the women brought initial reports of an empty tomb, the "words seemed to them an idle tale, and they did not believe them" (Luke 24:11). Jesus' talk of "going away," of "going back to his Father," might also have been taken less literally, interpreted—not unreasonably— simply as the death Jesus had now suffered already, the period during which his body had laid in the tomb. His *spirit* had gone away, perhaps, and had now returned. And now, since he had died already, the apostles may well have been hoping he'd never be parted from them again. This is why his words to the weeping Mary Magdalen came, possibly, as an unwelcome surprise: "Jesus said to her, 'Do not hold me, for I have not yet ascended to the Father; but go to my brethren and say to them, I am ascending to my Father and your Father, to my God and your God'" (John 20:17).

Before that ascension, however, Jesus still had two bits of unfinished business with individual apostles: Thomas and Peter.

"Doubting Thomas" seems a rather unfair moniker for the disciple surnamed *Didymus* (a Greek word meaning "a twin"), given that the other ten had just called the Resurrection "an idle tale" in his absence! Yes, when Jesus made his first post-resurrection appearance to the apostolic band, Thomas was away licking his wounds someplace. And yes, when given his own secondhand report, he blurted forth some very foolish words out of his hurt: "Unless I see in his hands the print of the nails, and place my finger in the mark of the nails, and place my hand in his side, I will not believe" (John 20:25). (Foolish indeed. Thomas, as one of the Twelve, had already seen at least *three* resurrections already: the raising of the widow's son, the raising of Jairus's daughter, and the raising of Lazarus).

Nevertheless, "doubting" Thomas now owns the everlasting glory to have gone, in the space of about two and a half verses, from refusing to believe at all to having earned the distinction of being the only person in the Gospels to address our Savior simply as "God" (John 20:28). Thomas's miracle, at any rate, may be profitably thought of as a bookend to that happy story with which we began our journey: Nathanael bar Tolmai's similar confession.

Peter, too, needed rehabilitation prior to the Ascension, having denied the Lord not as Judas did, out of rage and frustration, but purely from cowardice—terrified by a couple of teenage girls![63] And his subsequent shame was threatening to shipwreck God's plan for him to be chief of Christ's vicars on earth.[64] So Jesus submits him to a recertification test, as it were—a round of grueling examination. The risen Christ asked the fisherman three times, "Do you love me?"—one query for each of his denials in Caiaphas's courtyard, and each repetition more painful for Peter. With every rededication on Peter's part—"Lord, you know that I love you!"—the Good Shepherd solemnly repeats "Feed my

63 See Matt. 26:69-72.

64 In every single biblical list, Peter is named first. He is even called "first" at one point (Matt. 10:2), a word that, in its context, may justly be rendered as "chief." He preaches the first Christian sermon (Acts 2:14), works the first Church miracle (Acts 3:1-10), opens the first Church council (Acts 15:7), and takes the lead in filling Judas's empty spot in the apostolate. Whatever his later role may have been (or that of any successors), Peter certainly acts as spokesman for the group and seems to be recognized by them as such.

sheep" (John 21:15-17). Then the Lord walks away—like a baseball manager heading back to the dugout, having determined to leave his shaky starter on the hill at the conclusion of a spine-stiffening mound visit.

In the days leading up to the Ascension itself, all of the remaining Eleven received a round of recommissionings as well; and of all Gospel passages these tell us the most about Christ's special role for them in the new age to come. He had already "opened their minds to understand the scriptures" (Luke 24:45), at their initial reunion in the Upper Room, just as he had done for the Emmaus Road disciples. Already he had widened one of Peter's prerogatives to include the other ten: "Truly, I say to you, whatever you bind on earth shall be bound in heaven, and whatever you loose on earth shall be loosed in heaven" (Matt. 18:18).[65] This "binding and loosing" was a term that the Pharisees, "sitting in Moses' seat," used previously when commissioning legates of their own.

Finally, Jesus delegated the full authority of his own teaching office to the apostles. So that "repentance and forgiveness of sins should be preached in his name to all nations, beginning from Jerusalem" (Luke 24:47-48), he charged them with his great missionary mandate, "Go into all the world and preach the gospel to the whole creation. He who believes and is baptized will be saved; but he who does not believe will be condemned" (Mark 16:15-16). Once again, we see the dramatic necessity of an accompanying *supernatural guarantee* associated with their teaching: whoever does not accept the word of this small group of Galilean rustics . . . will be eternally lost!

Then Jesus added the "secret sauce" he had promised: "'Peace be with you. As the Father has sent me, even so I

65 Notice, however, that there is no mention of the keys in this verse.

send you.' And when he had said this, he breathed on them, and said to them, 'Receive the Holy Spirit. If you forgive the sins of any, they are forgiven; if you retain the sins of any, they are retained'" (John 20:21-23). Recall that this power to forgive sins on earth belonged to God alone. Now, Jesus opens a conduit for this same power to these, his vicars, so that it might still be exercised among men during his absence. And the evidences of this new unction were to be striking: "And these signs will accompany those who believe: in my name they will cast out demons; they will speak in new tongues; they will pick up serpents, and if they drink any deadly thing, it will not hurt them; they will lay their hands on the sick, and they will recover" (Matt. 16:17-18).

Finally, at the mount of the Ascension itself, "Jesus came and said to them, 'All authority in heaven and on earth has been given to me. Go therefore . . . " (Matt. 28:18-20).

Because I have all authority, that is, *you may go*—for Jesus has authority to give, authority that he is free to delegate, as he had already done once before when "he called to him his twelve disciples and gave them authority" Matt. 10:1). Among his last words on earth, then, is a reiteration of a gift already given, as basis for the apostles' global mission: "Go, therefore, and make disciples of all nations, baptizing them in the name of the Father and of the Son and of the Holy Spirit, teaching them to observe all that I have commanded you; and lo, I am with you always, to the close of the age" (Matt. 28:19-20).

St. Luke completes the story at the beginning of the book of Acts:

> He ordered them not to leave Jerusalem, but to wait there for the promise of the Father. "This," he said, "is what you have heard from me; for John baptized with water, but you will be baptized

> with the Holy Spirit not many days from now . . . [and] you will receive power when the Holy Spirit has come upon you; and you will be my witnesses in Jerusalem, in all Judea and Samaria, and to the ends of the earth." And when he had said this, as they were looking on, he was lifted up, and a cloud took him out of their sight. And while they were gazing into heaven as he went, behold, two men stood by them in white robes, and said, "Men of Galilee, why do you stand looking into heaven? This Jesus, who was taken up from you into heaven, will come in the same way as you saw him go into heaven" (1:4–11).

St. Mark includes the detail that "the Lord Jesus," having been taken up to heaven, "sat down at the right hand of God" (Mark 16:19).

Here finally, was the key to our great puzzling paradox. The apostles, thanks to the word of these two "men" (whom the Church has always understood to have been angels in human form), suddenly realized that they had just witnessed the end of Christ's *first coming* . . . which realization just happened to be necessary for grasping the idea that there would be a second. Like a big 1960s Bible movie at the intermission, the story was only half-finished. Once again, a thousand light bulbs clicked on, and a multitude of hitherto impenetrable parables—the landowner who went away to a far country, the thief who comes in the night, the wise and the foolish virgins—suddenly made perfect sense. But this second coming—this *parousia*, as the New Testament epistles will call it in Greek—was to be quite a bit different from the first.

The seed of the idea may be found in our Lord's very first sermon, way back at the synagogue in Capernaum. There, Jesus had unrolled the prophecy of Isaiah, chapter 61, using verse 1 to announce the start of his public ministry: "The Spirit of the Lord is upon me, because he has anointed me to preach good news to the poor. He has sent me to proclaim release to the captives and recovering of sight to the blind, to set at liberty those who are oppressed, to proclaim the acceptable year of the Lord" (Luke 4:18-19). And here, Luke tells us, our Savior stopped abruptly and rolled up the scroll.

Inspiring words, to be sure, and suggestive of great things to come . . . but for those really familiar with Isaiah's book, very noticeably *truncated* as well; cut-off in mid-sentence and at critical points. Jesus had chosen to push the "pause" button for some reason, midway through verse 2. The remainder of the phrase from Isaiah, after "to proclaim the acceptable year of the Lord," reads "and *the day of vengeance of our God*." As one exegete memorably expressed it, to the Jews at Capernaum this "would be like someone singing the national anthem and ending with, 'O'er the land of the free.' Everybody would be waiting for 'and the home of the brave.' But Jesus didn't finish the line. Jesus omitted the bit about 'the day of vengeance of our God.'"[xxxviii]

The rest of Isaiah 61 is a similarly strange mix of tenderness and justice cut straight. There will be comfort, writes the prophet, when the acceptable year arrives; comfort "to those who mourn in Zion . . . a garland instead of ashes, the oil of gladness instead of mourning" (vv. 2-3). Yet more than a few of these comforts will be comforting, it seems, because they feature that long-delayed element of *payback* against the enemies of God's family: "Aliens shall stand and feed your flocks, foreigners shall be your plowmen and vinedressers . . . you shall eat the wealth of the nations, and in their riches you shall glory. Instead of your shame you shall have a double portion, instead of dishonor you shall rejoice in your lot; therefore in your land you shall possess a double portion; yours shall be everlasting joy. For I the Lord love justice, I hate robbery and wrong; I will faithfully give them their recompense" (vv. 5-8).

And who is to bring this recompense? The one whom God has "covered with the robe of righteousness, as a bridegroom decks himself with a garland" (v. 10).[66]

Did Jesus stop halfway through verse 2 because, as some sentimentalists have taught, he didn't believe in judgment and came only to bring the Jubilee? One might very well think so, absent any glimpse of the bigger picture. After all, "God did not send the Son into the world to condemn the world, but in order that the world might be saved through him" (John 3:17), and "I do not judge anyone who hears my words and does not keep them, for I came not to judge the world, but to save the world" (John 12:47). Elsewhere in John, however, Jesus said, "The Father judges no one but has given all judgment to the Son, so that all may honor the Son just as they honor the Father . . . For just as the Father has life in himself, so he has granted the Son also to have life in himself; and he has given him authority to execute judgment, because he is the Son of Man" (John 5:22, 25-27). On various other occasions, our Lord owned up to his role as the judge of humanity very frankly: "For the Son of Man is going to come with his angels in the glory of his Father, and then he will repay each person according to what he has done" (Matt. 16:27), he said, and he warned that there "will appear in heaven the sign of the Son of Man, and then all the tribes of the earth will mourn" (Matt. 24:30).

Is there contradiction here? Only if we fail to factor in the *time element* involved, as some of the Essenes did in their

66 It should be noted that these dark-sounding prophecies can be read in a more positive light as well; the Gentiles are to be subjected, yes—to Israel's loving God. Once grafted into his kingdom, they will become the primary vinedressers and plowmen who, in the age of grace ahead, are to gather in a previously unimaginable harvest of souls. See also Isaiah 56:3-7, 60:3-7, 66:18-21.

curious efforts to resolve the conundrum back in the days of the Baptizer. These Qumranites gradually began "expecting two Messiahs, a priestly one from the line of Aaron and a royal one from the line of David," says John Bergsma. "They termed these two messiahs 'the Messiah of Aaron and the Messiah of Israel.'""[xxxix] It was this attempt to segregate Melchizedek's two offices—due to an inability to imagine one Savior saving in two distinct ways, during two distinct phases of his work—that gummed up most pre-Christian efforts to interpret Messianic prophecy. "But with the fulfillment of Christ's predicted birth, life, and labors," writes Lockyer, "the true solution became apparent that he was the one and only Messiah who came, first to suffer and afterwards to return and reign."[xl]

On the day of Pentecost, the Spirit whom Jesus imparted came with fullness and power . . . and began to make good on our Savior's promise in the Upper Room, the promise to guide the apostles into all truth (John 16:13). Now the apostles (twelve again, since the election of Matthias to fill the spot vacated by the traitor, Judas) used their delegated power to teach infallibly as their Master had done, to correctly interpret the data buried in the old prophecies—and, by the Spirit, to *make new prophecies of their own.*

"Behold," writes John to the churches of Asia, "he is coming with the clouds, and every eye will see him, even those who pierced him, and all tribes of the earth will wail on account of him" (Rev. 1:7).

Later in Revelation, John adds, "His eyes are like a flame of fire, and on his head are many diadems . . . He is clothed in a robe dipped in blood, and the name by which he is called is the Word of God. And the armies of heaven, arrayed in fine linen, white and pure, were following him on white horses. From his mouth comes a sharp sword with which to strike down the nations, and he will rule them with a rod of iron. He will tread the winepress of the fury of the wrath of God the Almighty. On his robe and on his thigh he has a name inscribed, King of kings and Lord of lords" (John 19:12, 13-18).

St. Jude quotes in his epistle an old extrabiblical prophecy long credited by the Jews: "'Behold, the Lord comes with ten thousands of his holy ones, to execute judgment on all and to convict all the ungodly of all their deeds of ungodliness that they have committed in such an ungodly way, and of all the harsh things that ungodly sinners have spoken against him" (Jude 1:14-15).

"The times of ignorance God overlooked," prophesies the new apostle Paul (not of the Twelve but also chosen by Christ personally[67]), "but now he commands all men everywhere to repent, because he has fixed a day on which he will judge the world in righteousness by a man whom he has appointed, and of this he has given assurance to all men by raising him from the dead" (Acts 17:30-31).

The "missing element" of vindication that had troubled so many remains troublesome today—even a barrier to faith for some. To this day, Jews who reject Jesus often do so because he has not brought about universal peace, or justice to Israel. If the Messiah has already come, they ask—how did the Holocaust happen?

Vindication is not missing, however, for those who have listened to the *whole* message of Christ: "These words [to the apostle John] are trustworthy and true, for the Lord, the God of the spirits of the prophets, has sent his angel to show his servants what must soon take place" (Rev. 22:6). "Soon" may seem a stretch to some, since John recorded his vision nearly 2,000 years ago. But on God's inhuman time scale, the happy ending that to the Church Militant seems so far

67 Acts 9 gives an account of St. Paul's separate calling.

off . . . is only a heartbeat away. It can be relied upon! "See, I am coming soon," says Christ the king; "my reward is with me, to repay according to everyone's work. I am the Alpha and the Omega, the first and the last, the beginning and the end" (Rev. 22:12).

Acts and the epistles show many proofs that the Twelve were quite aware they had received a special gift along with their commissioning. Peter, writing to all the churches in his second epistle, emphasizes the role of the apostles as *designated witnesses*—with the special credibility that entails:

> For we did not follow cleverly devised myths when we made known to you the power and coming of our Lord Jesus Christ, but we were eyewitnesses of his majesty. For when he received honor and glory from God the Father [at the Transfiguration] and the voice was borne to him by the Majestic Glory, "This is my beloved Son, with whom I am well pleased," we heard this voice borne from heaven, for we were with him on the holy mountain. And we have the prophetic word made more sure. You will do well to pay attention to this (2 Pet. 1:16-19).

A few paragraphs later, he seeks to remind the faithful "that you should remember the words spoken in the past by the holy prophets, and the commandment of the Lord and Savior spoken through your apostles" (2 Peter 3:2, NRSV). And Jude, in his short epistle, makes Peter's advice mandatory: "But you, beloved, must remember the predictions of the apostles of our Lord Jesus Christ" (1:17).

Paul's authority (fully endorsed, as it was, by the Twelve[68])

---

68 See Gal. 1.

was, because of the unique circumstances of his call, often challenged by dissidents. He defended himself forcefully—and on the same grounds: "Am I not an apostle? Have I not seen Jesus our Lord?" he protested (1 Cor. 9:1), and "The signs of a true apostle were performed among you with utmost patience, signs and wonders and mighty works" (2 Cor. 12:12). Neither is Paul shy about informing the erring Corinthians that "what I am writing to you is a command of the Lord" (1 Cor. 14:37).

How can that be? "[We] have received grace and apostleship to bring about the obedience of faith among all the Gentiles for the sake of his name," he writes to the Romans (1:4). For just "as we have been approved by God to be entrusted with the message of the gospel . . . we might have made demands as apostles of Christ. But we were gentle among you, like a nurse tenderly caring for her own children" (1 Thess. 2:4, 7). And it was Paul, too, who made explicit Peter's link between the authority of the prophets and that of the apostles—and the absolute necessity of that authority for building the Church: "So then you are no longer strangers and aliens, but you are citizens with the saints and also members of the household of God, built upon the foundation of the apostles and prophets, with Christ Jesus himself as the cornerstone" (Eph. 2:19-20).

Perhaps Scripture's most startling statement concerning apostolic authority is another of Jesus' own promises, made to the Twelve during his farewell discourse on Holy Thursday: "Truly, truly, I say to you, he who believes in me will also do the works that I do; and greater works than these will he do, because I go to the Father. Whatever you ask in my name, I will do it, that the Father may be glorified in the Son; if you ask anything in my name, I will do it" (John 14:12).

Is this to be taken literally?

That the apostles did the *same* works is easy to prove: in

Acts 9, Peter raised a dead woman; in Acts 3, he and John together caused a lame man to walk. And as with their Master himself, the miracles came in clusters: "many signs and wonders were done among the people by the hands of the apostles" (Acts 5:12); "a multitude gathered . . . and they were all healed" (Acts 5:15-16); "the rest of the people on the island who had diseases also came and were cured" (Acts 28:9). But can it really be true that the apostles did *greater* miracles than their Master?

It wasn't actually a competition, of course. As we have seen, Jesus himself gave them this power and willed it to continue after his departure ("these signs will accompany them . . . "). Augustine writes that when the apostles do greater works than Jesus, "it is all by his doing such works in or by them, and not as if they did them of themselves."[xli] Indeed, the statement is easier to accept once we recognize that the works done by Jesus on earth and the works done by the Holy Spirit after his ascension are both *the works of the same God*. Without the Spirit, the apostles were nothing . . . and *everyone* was without the Spirit before Christ opened the gates.

So, the same works, yes . . . but which works were greater, and in what sense? Several of the Fathers mention those who were healed simply because Peter's shadow passed over them (Acts 15:5), something never recorded of Jesus himself; or the sick and oppressed who were released by means of a handkerchief or other article of clothing that had been blessed by the hands of Paul (Acts 19:12). The great Anglican divine John Wesley (himself an avid student of the Fathers) got closer when he noted that "the converting of one sinner is a greater work than all these."[xlii] The greatest work of all was the work for which Christ had most directly called and empowered his Twelve—"Go into all the world and preach the gospel to the whole creation . . . make disciples of all nations, baptizing them in the name of the Father and of the Son and of the Holy Spirit."

Jesus wrote no Scripture while on earth. He never traveled more than 200 miles from tiny Bethlehem. While he was suffering, he had just one of his hand-picked disciples at his feet. But the idea that his kingdom would very start very small and then expand to almost unrecognizable proportions had been prophesied in his own Parable of the Mustard Seed: "The kingdom of heaven is like a grain of mustard seed which a man took and sowed in his field; it is the smallest of all seeds, but when it has grown it is the greatest of shrubs and becomes a tree, so that the birds of the air come and make nests in its branches" (Matt. 13:31-32).

The truly greater works, then, would be *works of conversion.*

When the Spirit came upon Peter on the day of Pentecost and he preached the world's first gospel sermon, "those who received his word were baptized, and there were added that day about three thousand souls" (Acts 2:41). Many of these converts were pagan Gentiles who had never even been part of Moses' covenant—a group that Jesus had declined to evangelize during his own ministry (""I was sent," he said in Matthew 15:24, "only to the lost sheep of the house of Israel").[69] Yet, by the year 150, St. Justin Martyr tells us that the Church had spread across the known world. By 250, perhaps a fifth of the entire population of the empire was Christian. And things only grew from there. "Christ

69 In God's economy of salvation, it was important that the Israelites, his covenant family, be given first dibs, so to speak. Just as God chose, in Abraham, one human family to become his disciples and then his ambassadors to the larger Gentile world, so Jesus redirects that family back to their missionary role in the persons of his Twelve (exclusively Israelite) apostles. It will be up to them to carry out this "greater work," Christ acting through them, having previously restricted his own earthly mission to the winning back of the original covenant family.

wrought miracles for two or three years in one country," writes Matthew Henry, "but his followers wrought miracles in his name for many ages in diverse countries . . . They should obtain greater victories by the gospel than had been obtained while Christ was upon earth. The truth is, the captivating of so great a part of the world to Christ, under such outward disadvantages, was the miracle of all."[xliii]

Those being evangelized understood very well where the power to accomplish these things came from. In Acts chapter 8, we see the wicked Simon Magus so convinced of the apostles' exclusive power to impart the Holy Spirit that he is willing to pay them money for their secret! And although it is outside the purview of this book to address the issues associated with apostolic succession, there is no question at all that Christ's chosen men took steps to ensure that our Lord's gifts for the building up of his Church should be passed down faithfully into the future, just as he passed them himself.[70]

As Paul told his own disciple, St. Timothy: "You then, my son, be strong in the grace that is in Christ Jesus, and what you have heard from me before many witnesses entrust to faithful men who will be able to teach others also" (2 Tim. 2:2). Earlier in that letter he reminded Timothy "to rekindle the gift of God that is within you through the laying on of my hands; for God did not give us a spirit of timidity but a spirit of power and love and self-control . . . Follow the pattern of the sound words which you have heard from me, in the faith and love which are in Christ Jesus; guard the truth that has been entrusted to you by the Holy Spirit who dwells within us" (2 Tim. 1:6-7, 13). And the same apostle told Titus, another of his own disciples whom he had left

70 These steps form the central theme in another of the author's books, *Four Witnesses; The Early Church in Her Own Words,* from Ignatius Press.

him behind at one of his mission works, to "amend what was defective [there], and appoint elders in every town as I directed you" (Titus 1:5).

This building-up of a worldwide episcopacy that has lasted two millennia, the perpetuation through time of the Lord's own principles of discipleship, is surely one of the greatest of the "greater works" of Christ's apostles.

Great, too, was their conscious exercise of the sweeping authority they had been granted. Almost certainly they had a role in determining the correct canon of the Old Testament for Christians. This was a matter the Hebrews had never actually settled; many different lists were in use among them—some lengthy, some decidedly shorter—with no universally recognized authority competent to settle the matter. The apostles also called and conducted the Jerusalem Council recorded in Acts 15, in order to determine the precise relationship between Jewish law-keeping and gospel liberty in a Church made up of both Gentiles and Israelites. Significantly, the apostles insisted that it was the *Spirit* announcing his verdict via their council (Acts 15:28).

Most impressive of all, perhaps, they presided over the passing of the Jewish Sabbath as the chief day set apart for the worship of Yahweh and made the "Lord's Day," the first day of the week, obligatory instead. It isn't quite correct to say that they *changed* the one to the other—rather, the one had died with Jesus at the cross and the other came to life independently and gradually supplanted it.[71] But certainly, the apostles set their seal to the change. Chosen by God to actually put their Master's lessons about the cessation of the

71 Many Christians of Israelite backgrounds continued to keep an optional Saturday Sabbath for at least ten years after Pentecost—perhaps even Peter himself, who we know from Acts 10 was still keeping kosher.

laws into effect, they rose to the occasion . . . and then took the heat (in the form of decades of persecution by the elders of the synagogue). "The universal and uncontradicted Sunday observed in the second century," notes patristics scholar Philip Schaff, "can only be explained by the fact that it had its roots in apostolic practice."[xliv]

There can be no doubt that the apostles' great work of evangelization took them to the ends of the earth. Of the eventual ends of the Twelve themselves, by which they glorified the God they served, there are many pious legends, several ancient histories that may include creditable material, and a few solid facts.[72] Those ends appear to have brought at least *eleven of the Twelve* to the place of self-sacrifice, as did

---

72 When approaching extrabiblical stories about Bible characters, it is always important to distinguish between the various senses of the word *tradition* and what the Church means by them. *Sacred Tradition* is that portion of the one deposit of faith left behind by the apostles and perpetuated in the Church distinct from the explicit notices of Scripture. The word is also often used by Catholics in a much less technical sense (with a lower-case "t," so to speak) when referring to venerable customs, long-standing folkways, and even widely accepted doctrines and practices that do not rise to the level of dogma. *Tradition* in this sense is something every religion has, and practically every human institution, in fact—from American jurisprudence to the concert halls of orchestral music. And often the word *traditional* can simply mean "old" or "deep-rooted" and may include stories about saints or notions about theology that are actually erroneous—or lacking, at least, a solid basis in the Church's genuine body of teaching. Confounding these three senses of the word can sometimes create the impression that the Church's teachings are being questioned or even attacked; for example, when historians or archaeologists reexamine some cherished aspect of extrabiblical hagiography, such as the legends of St. Christopher, for instance, that were, in fact, never actually taught as dogma by the Church. All this to say that hardly any of the extrabiblical stories about New Testament figures have ever been actually formally "taught" by the Church. This is why we can make serious attempts in good faith (as do the officers of the Church themselves) to distinguish between what real history we do find in the later records of the twelve apostles and the great mass of purely legendary material that has arisen, without becoming skeptics or "higher critics."

the saving purpose of their Master; while the last survivor lived long enough to bear personal witness until the dawn of the second century of the Christian dispensation.

The first to be lost (and the only apostle whose death is actually recorded within the pages of Scripture) was *James*, the elder brother of John—who never made it out of the home base of Jerusalem. James had once asked the Lord for a place at his right hand in the kingdom to come; Jesus asked him, "Are you able to drink the cup that I drink, or be baptized with the baptism that I am baptized with?" (Mark 10:38)—and his apostle, undaunted, replied in the affirmative. Jesus took him at his word, and James gained immortal glory by following his Savior's footsteps into the judgment hall of the Herods, where he received the same sentence of death (in his case, death by the sword—Acts 12:1-2).

Andrew and his brother *Simon Peter* got as far, respectively, as Byzantium and Rome—the two seats, interestingly, of the later division between Greek and Latin Christianity. Andrew planted the seeds of faith in Scythia, a region that corresponds today to Poland, Ukraine, and southern Russia, later reaching the modest town that became Constantine's "New Rome" on the Bosporus and being consecrated (according to the ninth-century historian Nicephorus) the first bishop of that city. His brother—conspicuously noted now for his bold evangelical courage—died at Old Rome on the Tiber; crucified upside down, according to Tertullian, in Nero's circus. Before that, he helped found the church at Antioch, where believers were first called "Christians"; then he undertook numerous missionary journeys before taking on his most famous job in Rome.

The post-Acts movements of *Philip*, who introduced Nathanael to Christ, are much more difficult to trace, owing to the hopeless confusion between himself and the Philip who is mentioned in Acts 21:8-9—another man entirely. Since this mix-up has been ongoing since the late second century, the many old tales of Philip's missionary adventures are, in the words of the *Catholic Encyclopedia*, "purely legendary and a tissue of fables."[xlv] The attractive story that depicts *Thomas* as the "apostle to India" is perhaps a bit less chancy, but only marginally so. The main problem is that the only real source for the story is an extravagant Gnostic document called *The Acts of Thomas*, which goes so far as to depict Thomas as Jesus' twin brother! It is true, however, that solid archaeological discoveries have verified some of the names cited in the book along with a few other historical details; so it is possible that a kernel of truth might be preserved underneath it all. The type of problems we find, at any rate, while examining the later careers of these two—Philip and Thomas—may be taken as illustrating the difficulties involved whenever the Church has attempted to nail down truly reliable material about the less famous names on the list.

The name of *Matthew/Levi* is certainly very prominent, though: author, as he was, of the Gospel from which we have gleaned so much of the story found in these pages. Yet Matthew's name, too, has generated a great many mutually contradictory legends, though a few of them may contain, here and there, some bits of truth. Some say he labored in Persia, Macedonia, and Syria; others in the area around the Caspian Sea. There is, at least, a solid tradition that he died a martyr—but whether he died on the block, at the stake, or stoned to death by the Jews, is impossible to determine. Our other "political" apostle, Simon Zealotes, hasn't fared much better in the biographical department; he may have reached Britannia in his travels, or Roman Egypt—he may even have been one of the earliest bishops of Jerusalem. The stories, again, are muddled and contradictory.

Jude Thaddeus, whose feast day the Western Church has combined with that of his co-worker Simon (October

28),[73] was, according to Eusebius, "said to have been the brother of the Lord according to the flesh." This is because many identify Jude (via a very complicated process) as the brother of "James the Just," whom Scripture definitely does peg as one of the "brethren of the Lord."[xlvi] (This would, incidentally, also make Jude the son of Clopas/Cleopas, one of the Emmaus Road disciples). His fate, at any rate, is no more clear than these other two with whom he has been grouped; he may have ministered in Samaria, Mesopotamia, and Libya. The admirable story of his death by means of an axe while on a preaching tour of Edessa is, alas, marred by another case of mistaken identity; he has, more than likely, been confused in that account with another disciple, Thaddeus of Edessa, one of the seventy.

It was *James* the Just who held down the Jerusalem phase of Jesus' final command: "Jerusalem, Judea, Samaria, and the ends of the earth." Both Scripture and history identify him as the man who spent his entire career as first bishop of the first local church in Christendom. St. Clement of Alexandria (writing about A.D. 210) tells us how the apostle earned his famous cognomen: "This James, whom the people of old called the Just because of his outstanding virtue, was the first, as the record tells us, to be elected to the episcopal throne of the Jerusalem church." Hegessipus, writing early in the second century, maintained that James had taken the vows of a Nazarite early in life—"he drank no wine nor strong drink, nor ate animal food, and no razor touched his head"—and continued to observe those strictures even as a Christian bishop. Scripture shows him co-presiding with Peter at the Jerusalem Council, and not long afterward we

73 *The Golden Legend* (from the thirteenth century) says, "Simon Cananean and Judas Thaddeus were brethren of James the Less and sons of Mary Cleophas, who was married to Alpheus."

find the newly converted Saul/Paul presenting himself to "the pillars of the Church" (Gal. 2:9) and listing the name of James along with Cephas (Peter) and John. The circumstances of his death are related by Eusebius in his *Church History* and also by the Jewish historian Josephus: "Albinus assembled the Sanhedrin of judges, and brought before them the brother of Jesus, who was called Christ, whose name was James, and some of his companions . . . and when he had formed an accusation against them as breakers of the law, he delivered them to be stoned."[xlvii]

Matthias, the "bench player" from among the seventy who stepped in when Judas faltered and failed, seems to have begun in Judea as well, but moved on to the region the Greeks called Colchis (at the intersection of eastern Europe and western Asia). An early legend says that he preached the gospel to "barbarians and cannibals" there, gave up his life, and was buried at Sebastopol. A second-century Gospel circulated in his name may or may not have been authentic; the version with which Clement, Origen, and Jerome were familiar was, however, condemned by them as tainted with Gnostic interpolations.

John bar Zebedee, brother of the greater James, traditionally held to be the beloved disciple who was faithful at the foot of the cross and to whose care Jesus commended the bereft *Mater Dolorosa*, Mary, lived to be nearly 100 years old. With Mary, he moved to Ephesus, where he planted churches and ministered to the whole region of Asia Minor for many decades. While there, he is traditionally held to have written the Gospel of John along with the three New Testament epistles that bear his name, and may have written the book of Revelation (after a strenuous sojourn at the Roman penal colony of Patmos). Among the Twelve, he was the last man standing.

Even in extreme old age, however, his experiences with

the Lord (which had happened when John was not much more than a teenager) seemed to him like yesterday. That which "was from the beginning," he writes in the first epistle, "what we [apostles] have heard, what we have seen with our eyes, what we have looked at and touched with our hands, concerning the word of life—this life was revealed, and we have seen it and testify to it . . . [W]e declare to you what we have seen and heard so that you also may have fellowship with us; and truly our fellowship is with the Father and with his Son Jesus Christ" (1 John 1:1-3). Near the end, when he had lost the ability to write (or even, according to tradition, to see or hear much of anything) John could still greet visitors, as St. Jerome tells us, with the same simple message, over and over: "Little children, love one another!"

We have not yet reached *Nathanael bar Tolmai*, with whom we began this journey. When Pantaenus, the great second-century theologian and apologist and mentor of Origen, really did reach India, he was told that Nathanael had been there first, some fifty to sixty years earlier. He had brought with him, the apologist heard with amazement, a copy of Matthew's Gospel written in Hebrew,[74] which was still treasured by the small body of Christians he encountered there. After founding that church, it was said, Nathanael traveled on to Armenia, a land of particular savagery

74 Many of the earliest Fathers assert the idea that St. Matthew wrote a Gospel in Hebrew; while the existing Matthew we find in the New Testament today was composed in Greek. Irenaeus, Origen, Eusebius, and Jerome all claim that this alleged Hebrew form was Matthew's original version prepared for his own use in evangelizing his fellow Israelites. Jerome (who appears to have had a copy on hand, since he uses it several times to resolve difficulties for his translation into Latin) states his belief that our canonical Greek version is a translation of the Hebrew original, though he does not know who did the translating or when. No copy has ever been found—and there is some possibility that Pantaenus and the others were mistaking the unrelated, non-canonical *Gospel According to the Hebrews* of the second century for this supposed Hebrew Matthew. The actual facts may never be known.

in those days. He converted the king there, a man named Polymius, angering the king's brother—who vowed to take revenge. Nathanael was captured and taken to a place of torture, where, on a rack, he was skinned alive with flaying knives. (He is often represented in Christian art—as in Michelangelo's *Last Judgment*—as flayed and holding in his hand his own skin). One version of the story relates that his murderers were perplexed that their victim, rather than cursing them in his agony or begging for release, sang a hymn instead commemorating Jesus Christ as Savior of the world. Even at the end our Nathanael was still testifying to his Master, with the complete knowledge now won by his long discipleship: "Rabbi, you are the Son of God! You are the king of Israel!" Not long afterward, Nathanael saw Jesus again face to face.

"The apostles," wrote the great Macarius of Egypt, "being themselves light, administered light to those who believed, enlightening their hearts with that heavenly light of the Spirit by which they themselves were enlightened."[xlviii] If we allow them to render us this service today, and if we embrace the light we receive from them, allowing it to chase our darkness, we too may stand one day at the pillars of the New Jerusalem and see their names inscribed.

By their diligence in preparing themselves under John the Baptist; by answering the call to discipleship when so many didn't; by receiving the same powers as their Master and employing them as he did for the building up of the kingdom; by accepting the burden of leading and interceding for God's people just as the twelve patriarchs once did—and succeeding where they failed; by their staggering at the mystery of the Incarnation—and their staying on anyway; by all these means our twelve apostles grew worthy of the special role for which their Savior worked so hard to prepare them. Acting as permanent, official witnesses to the gospel for the Church they helped found, the apostles more than earned their right to be called Christ's own ambassadors . . . the indispensable building blocks of the one *apostolic* Church and indeed the very foundations of heaven.

These Twelve saved the world—at the behest, of course, of the Thirteenth Man in their never-to-be-forgotten band of brothers. Thanks be to God.

You are the eternal Shepherd
who never leaves his flock untended.

Through the apostles you watch over us
and protect us always.

You made them shepherds of the flock
to share in the work of your Son.

—Preface I
Feasts of the Apostles

ENDNOTES

i *Catholic Encyclopedia*, "Essenes," https://www.newadvent.org/cathen/05546a.htm.

ii Hippolytus, *On the Apostles and Disciples*, https://www.newadvent.org/fathers/0524.htm.

iii Fulton J. Sheen, *The World's First Love* (New York; McGraw-Hill Book Company, 1952); pg. 111.

iv Homily XII on the Gospel of John.

v Maximus of Turin, quoted in ACCS NT Vol. IVa, pg. 96.

vi *Catholic Encyclopedia*, "Elijah," https://www.newadvent.org/cathen/05381b.htm.

vii John Bergsma, *Jesus and the Dead Sea Scrolls* (New York; Image Books, 2019), pg. 26.

viii Charles John Ellicott, *A New Testament Commentary for English Readers*, Vol. 1, (London; Cassell and Company Ltd., 1878), pg. 79.

ix J.B. Lightfoot, *St. Paul's Epistle to the Galatians* (London; MacMillan & Co. Ltd; 1896), pg. 93.

x John Bergsma, *Jesus and the Dead Sea Scrolls* (New York; Image Books, 2019), pg. 55.

xi Cyril of Alexandria, quoted in ACCS NT Vol. III, pg. 294.

xii Jerome, quoted in ACC NT, Vol 1a, pg. 191.

xiii Dave Armstrong, *Proving the Catholic Faith is Biblical* (Manchester NH; Sophia Institute Press, 2015), pg. 6.

xiv All Jefferson quotes taken from *The Jefferson Cyclopedia*, edited by John P. Foley (New York and London; Funk and Wagnalls Company, 1900).

xv *Catholic Encyclopedia*, "James," https://www.newadvent.org/cathen/08280a.htm.

xvi *Catholic Encyclopedia*, "Son of God," https://www.newadvent.org/cathen/14142b.htm.

xvii Ibid.

xviii Robert Hugh Benson, *Paradoxes of Catholicism* (New York, London, Bombay and Calcutta; Longmans Green and Company, 1913), pg. 46.

xix Herbert Lockyer, *All the Miracles of the Bible* (Grand Rapids, MI; Zondervan Publishing House, 1961), pg. 48.

xx John Chrysostom, ACCS, NT vol 1b, pg. 44.

xxi John Chrysostom, ACCS, NT vol 1b, pg. 45.

xxii Cyril of Jerusalem, ACCS NT Vol. Ib, pg. 55.

xxiii CCC 607.

xxiv Augustine, ACCS Mark, pg. 114.

xxv John Chrysostom, ACCS Mark, pg. 110.

xxvi Herbert Lockyer, *All the Apostles of the Bible* (Grand Rapids, MI; Zondervan Publishing House, 1972), pg. 166.

xxvii Cyril of Alexandria, ACCS NT Vol IVb, pg. 249.

xxviii *Catholic Encyclopedia*, "Judas Iscariot," http://www.newadvent.org/cathen/08539a.htm.

xxix Scott Hahn, *Reasons to Believe* (New York; Image Books, 2007), pg. 44.

xxx Tertullian, *Demurrer to the Heretics*, chap. 21, nos. 1–2, in FEF 1:120–21, no. 293.

xxxi Cyril of Alexandria, ACCS Vol III, pg. 173.

xxxii Note at Hebrews 7, *Ignatius Catholic Study Bible, New Testament* (San Francisco, Ignatius Press, 2010) pg. 425.

xxxiii Robert Grossteste, *On the Cessation of the Laws* (Washington, D.C.; Catholic University Press, 2012), pg. 229.

xxxiv Benedict XVI, *Jesus of Nazareth: From the Baptism in the Jordan to the Transfiguration* (New York; Image Books, 2007) pgs. 103-116.

xxxv All Benedict quotes in this section, including his citations from Rabbi Neusner, are taken from *Jesus of Nazareth: From the Baptism in the Jordan to the Transfiguration* (New York; Image Books, 2007) pg. 103.

xxxvi John Chrysostom, ACCS NT 1a, pg. 252.

xxxvii Origen, ACCS Matt. 1, pg. 250.

xxxviii Brian Zahnd, *Sinners in the Hands of a Loving God* (New York; Waterbrook/Crown Publishing, 2017) pg. 39.

xxxix John Bergsma, *Jesus and the Dead Sea Scrolls* (New York; Image Books, 2019), pg. 17.

xl Herbert Lockyer, *All the Messianic Prophecies of the Bible* (Grand Rapids, MI; Zondervan Publishing House, 1973), pg. 184.

xli Augustine, ACCS NT Vol IV, pg. 134.

xlii Wesley's Explanatory Notes, John 14:12, at https://www.biblestudytools.com/commentaries/wesleys-explanatory-notes/john/john-14.html.

xliii Matthew Henry's Commentary, John 14:12, at https://www.biblestudytools.com/commentaries/matthew-henry-complete/john/14.html.

xliv Rod: Schaff, Philip (1980 Reprint), *History of the Christian Church* (Grand Rapids, MI: Eerdmans), Vol. I., pg. 118.

xlv *Catholic Encyclopedia*, "Philip the Apostle," https://www.newadvent.org/cathen/11799a.htm.

xlvi For a complete exposition of this theory, see *Catholic Encyclopedia*, "St. James the Less," https://www.newadvent.org/cathen/08280a.htm.

xlvii *Antiquities* 20:9:1(197-203).

xlviii *Fifty Spiritual Homilies of Macarius the Egyptian*, trans: A.J. Mason (New York; MacMillan & Co., 1921) pg. 84.

ABOUT THE AUTHOR

Rod Bennett is the author of *Four Witnesses: The Early Church in Her Own Words*, widely considered to be a modern classic of Catholic apologetics; continuously in print for the last twenty years and a life-changing watershed for hundreds of spiritual inquirers. He is also a familiar voice on Catholic media outlets such as Ave Maria Radio and on popular programs like *Catholic Answers Live!* and Marcus Grodi's *Journey Home*. Rod's other books include *The Apostasy that Wasn't*, *The Christus Experiment*, and *Scripture Wars*. A convert from Evangelical churches, Rod joined the Catholic Church in 1996. He lives in the Great Smoky Mountains of Tennessee with his wife of thirty years, Dorothy.